TRANSFORMING
WHILE
PERFORMING

"Are today's digital transformations the twins of the reengineering projects of the '90s? Many of today's digital projects run that same risk as they merely replace previous applications with cloud equivalents. They generate lots of noise and require significant investment, but deliver disappointing payback. Impactful digital projects, in contrast, rethink business models, create smarter products and services, truly reshape the customer experience, and automate lots of dull, dirty, and dangerous tasks. *Transforming While Performing* focuses on the talent dimension to make you think very differently about the human element—and how to organize it in the book's elements of pods, guilds, and co-creation partner relationships. This book will force you to examine your internal and external talent pools and not just pave the old cow paths in your digital transformation."

—VINNIE MIRCHANDANI, Advisor, Author, Former Gartner Analyst, Deal Architect, Inc.

"Twenty-five years after the Netscape browser ushered in the era of digital transformation, industry analysts claim only 25 percent of global sales are digital while a mere 5 percent of firms are 'digital leaders.' Andres Angelani's *Transforming While Performing* is a pragmatic, seven-part manifesto that offers keen insight into how business executives must leverage digital technology to meet, and exceed, customer needs. It is a must read for business leaders intent on transforming their firm into digital."

—GARY BEACH, Publisher Emeritus of *CIO* magazine and a columnist for the *Wall Street Journal* CIO Journal

"*Transforming While Performing* outlines and ties together many of the essential capabilities needed to benefit from digital efforts. The capabilities linked together include: co-creation with diverse mind-sets, guilds/communities of talent, staff and effort nurturing as well as ongoing engagement in continuous improvement, customer-focused and human-connected design, and tolerance of failing fast and the need to partner. Executives taking on the digital challenge should compare their enterprise's capabilities and real execution against those suggested in the book, as well as consider how well they are linked within their enterprise."

—BRUCE J. ROGOW, President, IT Odyssey & Advisory

"Every established organization confronts the digital transformation imperative; yet the road ahead is perilous. In *Transforming While Performing*—the title clearly specifies the challenge—Andres Angelani shares crucial lessons for how to navigate into the future: building strategic partnerships, developing internal competencies, and building a culture of innovation."

—VIJAY GURBAXANI, Director, Center for Digital Transformation and Taco Bell Endowed Professor of Information Systems and Computer Science at the University of California, Irvine

"Can such a spirit of unfettered innovation last in today's data-intensive digital era? Yes, and more so, says Andres Angelani, CEO of Cognizant Softvision. In his book, *Transforming While Performing: A Practical Guide to Being Digital*, Angelani says digital helps open the gates of rapid, fail-fast type of innovation. He outlines the key elements of innovation: starting with a gamification approach to meeting objectives, along with a design approach to management."

—JOE MCKENDRICK, *Forbes* Contributor, Independent Author and Analyst

"In *Transforming While Performing*, Angelani writes, 'The ability to interact with another person or in a group is innately human.' While technology continues to develop at a breakneck pace, and companies search for better, more cost-effective ways to build their business, Angelani uniquely understands that companies and brands need to connect with their customers and each other on a human level."

—DAWN PRATT, Tech Up for Women

"To transform while you perform seems impossible until you realize that whenever you truly focus on your customers and their challenges—that is precisely what happens. Designing customer experiences, collaborating with partners to meet customer needs gets us out of our performance myopia and into the service mind-set that is core to succeeding in our digital age. Andres's latest book can help show you the way."

—GEOFFREY MOORE, Author, *Crossing the Chasm* and *Zone to Win*

A PRACTICAL GUIDE TO *BEING* DIGITAL

TRANSFORMING
WHILE
PERFORMING

How to create a culture of innovation with partners

ANDRES ANGELANI

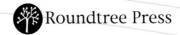
Roundtree Press

Text and photographs copyright © 2019 Cognizant Softvision
Cartoons copyright © 2019 @marketoonist.com; pages 19, 35,
59, 83, 111, 133, 155

Library of Congress Cataloging-in-Publication Data available.

ISBN: 978-1-944903-60-2

10 9 8 7 6 5 4 3 2

Manufactured in China

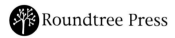
Roundtree Press

149 Kentucky Street, Suite 7
Petaluma, CA 94952

www.roundtreepress.com

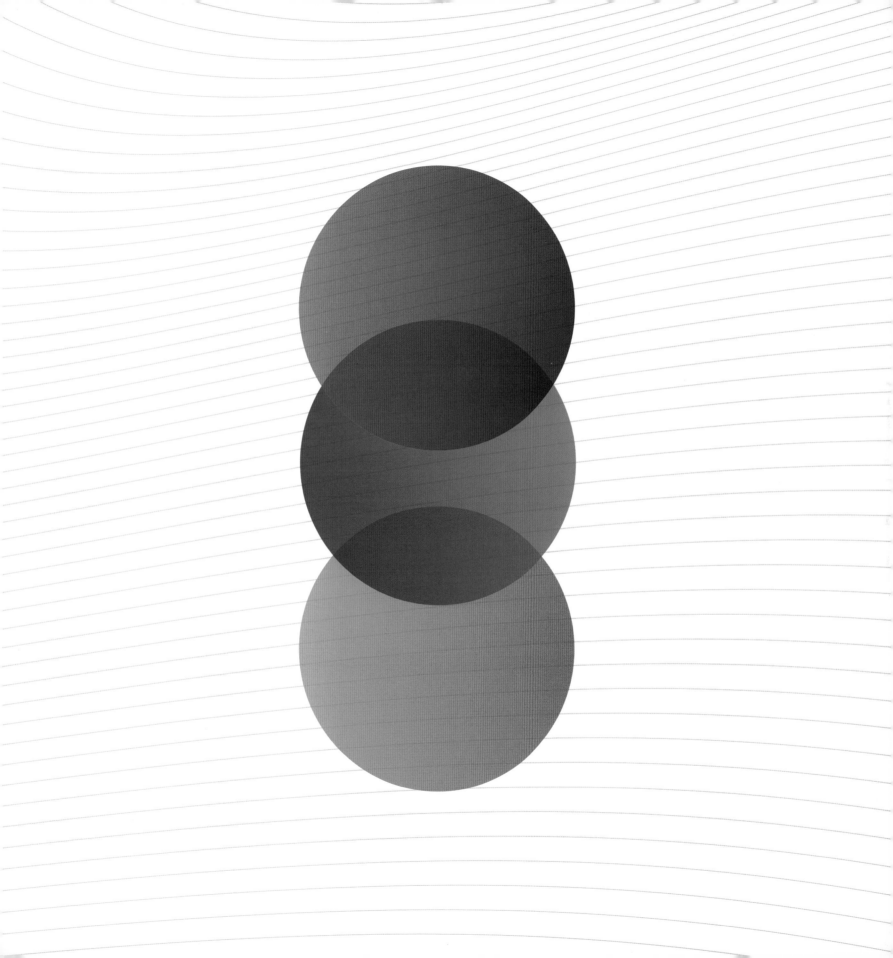

TABLE OF CONTENTS

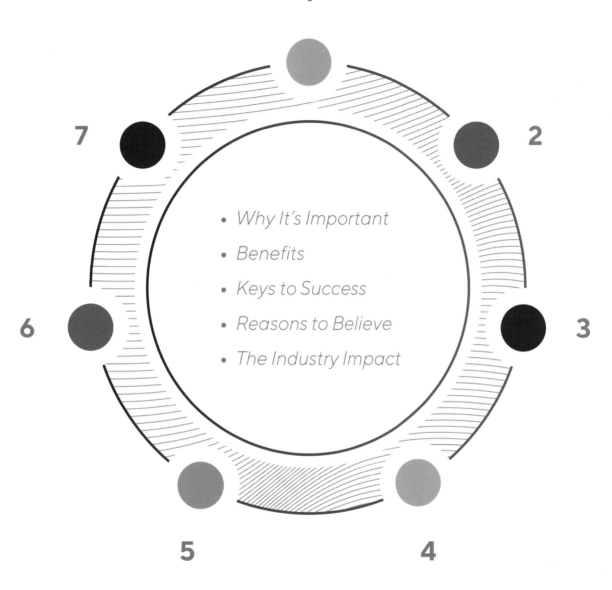

1

2

7

- *Why It's Important*
- *Benefits*
- *Keys to Success*
- *Reasons to Believe*
- *The Industry Impact*

3

6

5

4

FOREWORD

With all apologies to the word *innovation*, "digital" is likely the most overused and misunderstood word in business today. It has become a catch-all word, meaning all things to all people. In fact, forget the question you're looking to answer, because I already know the answer, and the answer is digital.

For years, digital was a channel, likely a means to engage audiences in new and different ways. Digital used to mean a cool and "sticky" website, and that evolved to an ecommerce platform, and that led to apps and experiences and all sorts of new and unique tools and ways to capture attention, loyalty, and revenue.

Sure, digital can be all those things, but it goes deeper still.

What Digital Isn't

Let's talk for a minute about what digital is not. Digital is not a channel. It isn't a clamped-on strategy, project, or practice. Digital is not a thing. And while digital can be construed as the opposite of analog, that's a pretty basic definition these days. Also, digital certainly involves technology and engagement, and represents a newish way of doing business. But this is more of a piecemeal definition that can lead to confusion, misalignment, and most importantly, missed opportunities.

What Digital Is

Digital is more about who, how, and why than what. It represents a philosophy and the DNA at the heart of an organization. Digital is a way of doing things. It's reimagining an entirely new way to do business and go to market, with customer and technology at the center.

It's much easier for smaller startup businesses to be digital than larger incumbent businesses. This is largely due to legacy technology and legacy thinking that often weigh down businesses and leadership teams.

Companies and organizations must have a thoughtful and sustainable approach to digital. That's where *Transforming While Performing: A Practical Guide to Being Digital* can be instrumental.

The book helps to establish a foundation and road map for what it means to be digital and to embark on this journey.

This foundation enables leadership teams to align, share a common vision, and ultimately work together to unlock and capture value and growth now.

INTRODUCTION

—

Maximizing Your Digital
Transformation Experience

IDC estimates that 40% of all technology spending will go toward digital transformations, with enterprises spending in excess of $2 trillion by 2019. It may be hard to believe that $2 trillion will be spent this year alone on digital transformation, especially considering that everyone seems to have a different definition of what we mean by the term "digital transformation."

- For many C-suite executives, digital transformation is all about process — a new type of formula for using digital technologies to create new business models, revenue streams, and a method to address the changing business environment and market dynamic.
- For others, it's an opportunity to use "in the moment" language to surround many modern innovation efforts, an all-encompassing term that captures the move away from legacy technologies and systems toward more agile software development and cloud/hybrid-cloud computing.
- And still for others, digital transformation is exactly that — the transformation of an organization designed to realign the business's respective models and proficiencies to help that organization (with all apologies to the United States Marine Corp) improvise, adapt, overcome, and better position itself for current and future growth opportunities.

So, are any of these more true than the others? Probably not, as these are all pretty accurate definitions and largely applicable to any organization looking to shift its thinking and business.

Still, the real answer as to which is the best definition likely rests within the organization itself, the mindset of its management team, and the objectives and outcomes it expects when embarking on its digital transformation.

A global cosmetics company with a history of pioneering new trends and technologies pivots and embraces digital partnerships, enabling the company to build market share, boost efficiency, establish a reputation in the new landscape of all things digital, and burnish the company's legendary status as beauty expert and leader.

To create a new kind of consumer bank, one that would appeal to the younger masses and be just a "swipe right" away at all times, one conservative financial institution went through a complete makeover, trading in its Brooks Brothers and wingtips wardrobe for hoodies, ripped jeans, and sneakers. The resulting successful transformation projects a more engaging Silicon Valley startup instead of a formal, buttoned-up bank.

A popular music provider barely ten years old intentionally created an environment where failure was taken as an opportunity to learn, innovate, and change. To transform the organization, teams brought design and technology together in a natural way with a measurement and incentive system that helped drive and reward behavior.

Three separate examples of digital transformation, each resulting in tremendous growth and success.

A closer look at each reveals three commonalities:

- Digital transformations begin and end with the **customer** at the center of everything.
- A nurturing and curious **culture** encourages continuous and sustainable innovation.
- The mindset and intelligence to embrace and **collaborate** with partners that bring new thinking and skill sets that would enable them to reach new heights together.

Today's digital transformation definitions have led to too many words, too much complexity, and way too much confusion. That's why we wrote *Transforming While Performing*: so that companies and executives who are in the process of or considering undertaking some form of digital transformation can better understand what that entails, and how to get the most out of the experience.

Two trillion dollars is no laughing matter, and this book is meant to be a guide for any reader at any business level, digital and nondigital, who is looking for a partner to help them understand what's most important and the necessary steps when embarking on a digital transformation strategy.

Digitally transforming your business for tomorrow doesn't mean you need to bring business to a halt and stop performing for today. *Transforming While Performing* is told through a partner's mindset, one that can help transform your business for today's all-digital environment.

A NEW ERA

In this new digital era that some call the "Fourth Industrial Revolution," companies are facing agile competitors that move into their established marketplaces fast, often disrupting and overtaking them with sophisticated strategies. The business ecosystem is getting larger and more complex, both in terms of technology and stakeholders. Whether it's a bank trying to navigate digital transformation and how it fundamentally challenges its business model, or a brick-and-mortar consumer retail business trying to build an online presence, partnerships are at the heart of bridging these wide gaps.

Companies and organizations have been busy adapting to the new normal of digital transformation sweeping across industries and markets. Many businesses have already built out their digital presence with varying degrees of success and failure. One common problem that IT departments encounter as part of their digital journey is embracing agile strategies that don't lead to the benefits and improvements they originally sought.

It is a fairly common problem for company executives to spend considerable budgets on agile enablement programs, only to find that they have not achieved the desired results. What's more, it has also led to confusion among company employees and partners alike, whereby teams are pulled between two very different points of focus: one that's driven by requirements and tight planning, and the other driven by a libertarian and noncommittal philosophy.

Nowhere is the postmortem of troubled digital partnerships more evident than in agile software-development projects. It is common for a partner's myopic adherence to agile technologies to obfuscate their awareness of the importance of creating value. This kind of issue gets exacerbated in partnerships where players are not connected to the overall business goals and just start building software without really caring or assessing the business impact of the new work.

Much of the time, companies approach their digital challenges in one of three ways: building their own technology, buying technology and talent through the acquisition of a strong digital player, or finding an aligned partner that can synergistically help them grow and benefit from the combined strengths of both companies.

In this new era of companies driving to transform all aspects of their business, they are discovering that they have great difficulty trying to accomplish the transformation without outside help. And the problems mentioned above around agile projects are clear examples of where partnership alignment with the correct skill sets and approaches would render better outcomes.

According to Noam Wasserman, a professor at Harvard Business School who studied almost ten thousand founders for his book *The Founder's Dilemma*, business partnerships can bring a company either triumphant glory or catastrophic disaster. Ideally, partners contribute diverse skills and talents to their business, providing a sense of wholeness that no one partner could have achieved alone.

Several decades before the Digital Revolution was in motion and companies were pressed to embrace digital transformation, business partnerships were as common as P&Ls. Surprisingly, many of the same concepts used in older business partnerships resonate with today's digital partnership approaches. In Rosabeth Moss Kanter's 1984 *Harvard Business Review* article, "Collaborative Advantage: The Art of Alliances," she outlined three basic criteria that fit today's partnering strategy nicely.

1. **Self-analysis:** Relationships get off to a good start when partners know themselves and their industry, and when they have assessed changing industry conditions and decided to seek an alliance.
2. **Chemistry:** This involves highlighting the personal side of business relationships but not denying the importance of sound financial and strategic analyses.
3. **Compatibility:** The courtship period tests compatibility on broad historical, philosophical, and strategic grounds: common experiences, values and principles, and hopes for the future.

But for today's digital partnerships to be effective, they need to be approached and integrated correctly. Over the past five years, in an era of radical changes in how consumers learn, explore, and buy products online, many of the world's largest companies have struggled with their digital strategies and partnerships.

When such a network of partnerships is integrated well, it can create a "transformational partnership" that helps participating parties gain insights, build greater customer traction, and execute their strategies in a way that is thoughtful and results in both parties gleaning new perspectives about their customers and market opportunities.

Our book, *Transforming While Performing*, focuses on the third path of combining partner strengths — transformational partnerships — as the most effective engine of growth. We will cover the elements required to build and realize transformational partnerships and all the benefits they provide to the company. Our goal is to provide executives and business owners with the key approaches and strategies that help establish and maintain transformational partnerships in this digital age.

We've arrived at this phase of our digital economy after many decades, in which human society and culture swiftly progressed from mechanical and analog electric technology to a ubiquitous landscape of interconnected digital technologies. It has been touted as the Digital Revolution. To anyone paying attention, it was clear that change was coming in accelerated bursts, and it was becoming ever harder to keep pace with the technology driving the transformation.

The fast-changing digital landscape, and the technologies driving it, have helped open doors for newcomers and created significant obstacles for incumbents to overcome. The new digital theater of interacting with customers and engaging them has confounded businesses that had been prospering for more than fifty years.

TRANSFORMATIONAL PARTNERSHIPS CAN WIELD DISRUPTIVE POWER

Why Partner in the Digital Era?

Partnering in the digital age is essential for companies lacking core digital culture and skills to build the products and experiences that help establish a stronger presence in the marketplace and lead to new opportunities. Achieving multidimensional digital capabilities comes about from four key elements derived from transformational partnerships:

1. **Access to specialized digital talents**
2. **Cross-pollination of experiences across industries**
3. **Reinforcing or creating the digital DNA of each company by leveraging strengths**
4. **Adopting a more agile process and a product mindset**

The fundamental takeaway from the discussion that follows in this book centers around how a partner ecosystem can convert nontech, industry-specialist players into an innovative and tech-savvy force that helps them achieve their digital-transformation goals.

For those companies that can't up their digital game, the stakes are great. In today's cosmetics markets, for example, there's a very short window of only five seconds for companies to capture an online customer.

Perhaps no other company in history has pivoted better than Netflix. Originally designed as a disruptive, yet marginally successful postal DVD rental service, Netflix has transformed itself and is now at the center of the home entertainment experience, upending the entertainment industry and forever changing the consumption of content.

Netflix has been so successful, it's often considered directly responsible for declining cable viewership, fewer television subscriptions, and less-effective traditional advertising models. It has spent billions developing original content, while also securing distribution rights for films and television shows. Its success has led to criticism from the cinema heavyweights, and Netflix films are banned from the Cannes Film Festival competition.

To become market leaders, companies are compelled to act quickly to seize the market of opportunity. This velocity can be achieved through transformational partnerships.

By transforming itself from a postal DVD service and revolutionizing film and television viewing, Netflix has brought more content to more people than anyone had ever imagined. It has opened the door for smaller, independent films and enabled more global reach via its streaming platform.

Netflix has also received its fair share of criticism, with fingers pointing to its recommendations system, which attempts to personalize everyone's viewing experience. Still, this and other complaints could be viewed as sour grapes by an industry that didn't transform quickly enough and that's been left watching Netflix eat its lunch with a transformative home-entertainment experience and platform.

Many companies have been blindsided by the abrupt changes of the Digital Revolution, and found themselves trying to play catch-up in how they approach and embrace today's digital technologies. Most have discovered that they're not alone, and fewer have figured out that they can progress and evolve by striking new partnerships that help them address their digital shortcomings. We hope this book will help you and your business navigate the challenges ahead and equip you with the transformational-partnership mindset that enables your company to realize its full potential and succeed.

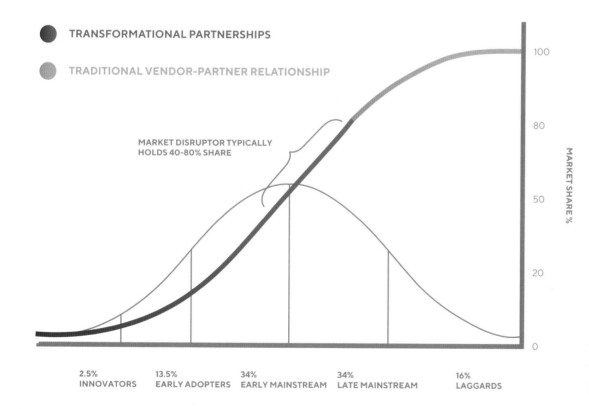

● **TRANSFORMATIONAL PARTNERSHIPS**

● TRADITIONAL VENDOR-PARTNER RELATIONSHIP

MARKET DISRUPTOR TYPICALLY
HOLDS 40-80% SHARE

MARKET SHARE %

100

80

50

20

0

2.5%
INNOVATORS

13.5%
EARLY ADOPTERS

34%
EARLY MAINSTREAM

34%
LATE MAINSTREAM

16%
LAGGARDS

THE PARTNERSHIP JOURNEY

Creating a Culture
of Partnership

CHOOSING A TECH PARTNER IS LIKE CHOOSING A MATE

Smart enterprises reach out to their partners and share risks and rewards while keeping their minds focused on the same vision.

HIGH-VALUE PARTNERSHIPS

An innovation culture requires all parties involved to have a shared vision and set of values where there's mutual benefit that goes far beyond the transactional monetary exchange in a business contract.

"True collaboration is much more than a purchase order," wrote Benjamin Gomes-Casseres in his *Harvard Business Review* article, "Partnership is Not a Purchase Order." "True collaboration always has open-ended elements — ranging from precisely how new innovations will be implemented, to how products will fare in the market, and even to what priorities partners will pursue in the face of changes in the environment."

We believe a "value partnership" is innovation-driven, distributed, and participatory. And that translates to all companies — whether they're big or small, successful or not. Innovation agility is not a solitary venture. This applies to products developed in partnership ecosystems as well as in the partnership's business model and governance.

As software becomes the business, the various stacks that make up a product and a go-to-market strategy exponentially increase in complexity. As a consequence, companies struggle to build up the skills, hire the right people, retain them, and build an agile operational system that drives sustainable innovation.

——

A shared vision and set of values should be mutually beneficial and go far beyond the short-term business transaction.

——

True collaboration always has open-ended elements. Trust is not prescriptive.

——

A "value partnership" is innovation-driven, distributed, and participatory.

PARTNERSHIP EVOLUTION: ONE TEAM, ONE METHOD, ONE CULTURE

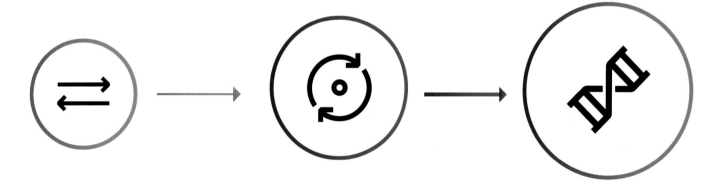

Transactional

- Tactical delivery
  to prescribed
  requirements

Agile

- Process and
  communication focus
- Flexible model
- Technical proficiency

Transformational

- Driven by business outcomes
- Talent development
- Market disruption
- Cocreation
- Product, design, and
  engineering combined

A COCREATION MINDSET FOSTERS INNOVATION

Why It's Important

Innovating with partners makes good business sense because a high-value partnership reduces cost, provides access to diverse talent and ideas, adds agility and speed, and increases differentiation in the marketplace.

For companies that want to change the course of their business, they do so in a coordinated fashion by gaining valued and trusted business partners, uncovering insights, innovating, making strategic and bold business decisions, and taking action together.

In today's rapidly evolving marketplace, where change is the only invariant, the company needs these actions to be impactful. It needs partners who take responsibility, make tough decisions, take political heat, innovate, and truly own the results.

When partners embrace a collective vision, they bring a diverse array of multidisciplinary skill sets and provide the basic ingredients to grow an innovation culture. Once the vision has been forged for a mutually beneficial relationship, the partnership starts to grow and evolve. One of the outcomes of these innovation-driven collectives is that they help establish a codevelopment mindset that enhances and extends the benefits beyond typical vertical, stovepipe engagements focused on solitary, transactional objectives.

However, organizations and individuals who try to transform on their own do so at their own risk. The prospects for success become marginal, especially without the right talent, experience, or partners.

Innovating with partners reduces costs, provides access to talent and ideas, and adds agility and speed.

Partners must take responsibility, make tough decisions, take political heat, innovate, and truly own the results.

The real threat lies in pursuing transformation without the right partner. In this scenario, the prospect for success becomes marginal, especially without internal talent or experience.

Miami Studio: Working together with our partners.

Benefits

Partnership longevity and success are built on trust. With those forces at work, leadership emerges as a direct outcome of the synergy between the two groups. Vision and leadership come together and create an X factor whereby new discovery happens for both companies. It triggers teams and groups to rally around, reinforcing the company's focus to grow and evolve.

Trust in partnership values also creates a culture of giving and contributing more than what is written in a business contract. It goes beyond individual successes and failures and toward making positive and continuous impact.

And these points are echoed by experienced CEOs who have been down this road many times with great success. According to Ray Zinn, the longest-serving CEO in Silicon Valley, "A stark reality that many ignore is that choosing a tech partner is like choosing a mate. You are creating a mutually dependent relationship."

Partners understand how powerful it can be to have a truly diverse team — diverse in style, in nationality, in gender, in life, and in business experience. They also understand how hard it can be to bring and to keep such teams together, how easy it is to take shortcuts under pressure of the market demands and project deadlines, and how tiresome it can be to continually display the leadership that binds the teams together and reminds them of the true value of partnership. But in true partnerships, where the dynamics, roles, and responsibilities are understood and embraced, the participants don't let those pressures get in the way of their work. They make it their mission to fight for diversity as well as the time and resources to build a productive balance where individual qualities and strengths are maximized to create agility and new business outcomes.

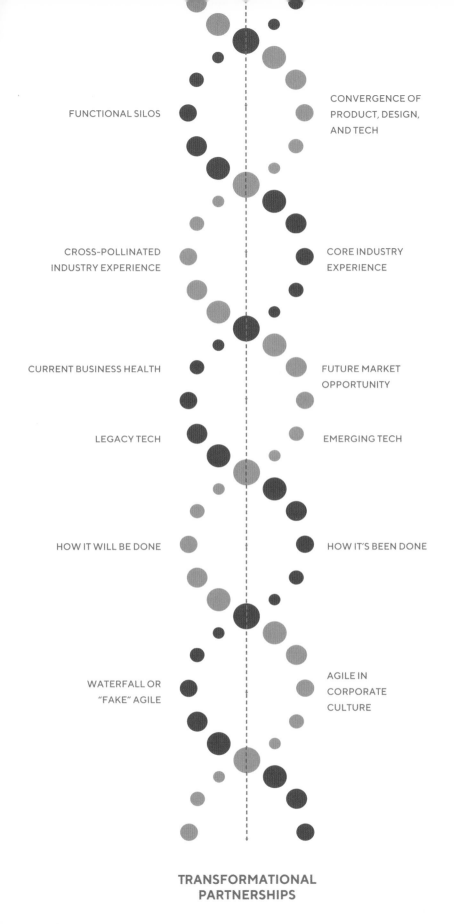

FUNCTIONAL SILOS

CONVERGENCE OF PRODUCT, DESIGN, AND TECH

CROSS-POLLINATED INDUSTRY EXPERIENCE

CORE INDUSTRY EXPERIENCE

CURRENT BUSINESS HEALTH

FUTURE MARKET OPPORTUNITY

LEGACY TECH

EMERGING TECH

HOW IT WILL BE DONE

HOW IT'S BEEN DONE

WATERFALL OR "FAKE" AGILE

AGILE IN CORPORATE CULTURE

TRANSFORMATIONAL PARTNERSHIPS

DIVERSITY CREATES INNOVATORS' DNA

Vision, trust, and leadership come together and create an X factor for partnerships.

A partnership whose main driver is the business outcome produced can outlive apparent cultural incompatibilities among tech partners and more traditional enterprises.

Talent diversity, functional convergence, and business-goal sharing are key principles to support a unified vision.

THE PARTNERSHIP FRAMEWORK

Walk Before You Run

Create a joint operating agreement

- Define a balanced governance model to motivate partners to give their best.
- Establish clear goals, roles, and responsibilities among partners and their leadership.

Cross-Pollinate

- Organize talent into communities to foster environments of natural collaboration, sharing, and learning.
- Create the foundation for trust bonds to form.

Leverage diversity–collapsing silos

- Allow people to work together in pursuing a goal that is visible enough to run above direct managerial mandate. Support the goal of the partnership from the very top in both companies.

Reward micro-improvements while setting larger and more challenging goals

- Adjust as you go.
- Be creative at rewarding.
- It's not just about the money.

Set a simple, short-term key performance indicator (KPI) system to measure outcomes

- Always measure and communicate; discuss how to improve often.

Model financial rewards out of relevant business outcomes

- Incentivize partners to invest.

Reasons to Believe

P artnerships don't stop when projects are done and the new products are launched. True partners continue to innovate to stay relevant.

In today's fast-moving digital marketplace, companies initiating new digital products or services don't have the luxury of time. Businesses must incorporate new products and technologies swiftly and in parallel to ongoing commerce activities. No company wants to hit the pause button on revenue-generating services or products. This, again, compels companies to think about the power of building a strong partnership whereby both parties are mutually in sync with the same objectives.

This is not just about financial success. It is about enhancing reputation, giving back to the community, and developing teams with each project. If these aims are kept in sight and continually furthered, the mission for long-term partnership is accomplished.

TRUE PARTNERS CONTINUE TO INNOVATE TO STAY RELEVANT

Businesses must incorporate new products and technologies swiftly and in parallel to ongoing commerce activities.

Think about the power of building a strong partnership whereby both parties are mutually in sync with the same objectives.

It is about enhancing reputation, giving back to the community, and developing teams with each project.

THE WINDOW OF OPPORTUNITY IS CLOSING

The Industry Impact

Stakeholders are in different geographies and time zones, and feel the pressure every day to grow and evolve their business. All of which means partnerships are expected to continue playing an essential role in driving digital business opportunities across the world. And the opportunity involves defining outcome-based compensation structures to incentivize partners to cooperate based on results and unite on business purposes.

1

"In 2018, **Amazon represented 39.7% of all online retail sales**, and is expected to reach 50% by 2023."

According to FTI Consulting, 2018 U.S. Online Retail Forecast

———

Growth is nurtured and supported by an innovation culture.

———

Partnerships are expected to continue playing an essential role in driving global digital business.

———

The opportunity involves defining outcome-based compensation structures to incentivize partners to cooperate based on results.

GUILDS

—

Building Communities
of Talent

MAKING PEOPLE THE NUMBER-ONE PRIORITY

Long-term success — even sustainability — of a partnership requires consciously setting up an internal organization that focuses on people. Communities are the most scalable model for talent development.

THE POWER OF THE COMMUNITY

A community is defined as a body of persons of common, and especially professional, interests scattered through a larger society. Traditional guilds build on the idea of community as an assemblage of skilled individuals organized around specific disciplines. Communities can layer on top of the organization's existing functional areas. Successful partnerships thrive when the skills and resources of talented individuals and teams are connected within a sustainable community structure that allows the group to evolve and grow. Take, for example, the Mozilla Project, which was launched at Netscape in 1998 and created the Mozilla Firefox Web browser through a community-based project.

Firefox has survived fierce competition, and despite being a nonprofit and resource-constrained, it symbolizes a free Internet and consistently ranks as one of the top-three global browsers. Today, it competes side by side with wealthy giants like Google's Chrome and Apple's Safari. Community has been key to its success.

Traditional guilds build on the idea of community as an assemblage of skilled individuals.

Partnerships thrive when the skills and resources of talented individuals and teams are connected within a sustainable community.

Communities should nurture talent and help it grow.

A GUILD CONNECTS COMMUNITIES ACROSS GEOGRAPHIES AND ORGANIZATIONAL BOUNDARIES

Inside the Artificial Intelligence Guild

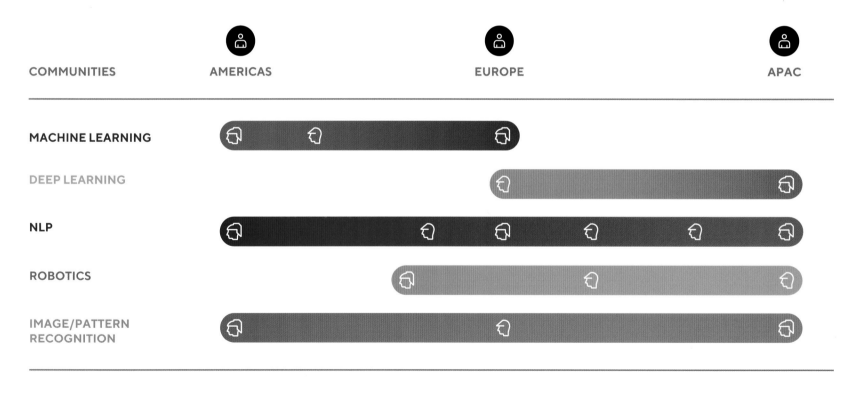

COMMUNITIES	AMERICAS	EUROPE	APAC
MACHINE LEARNING			
DEEP LEARNING			
NLP			
ROBOTICS			
IMAGE/PATTERN RECOGNITION			

 COMMUNITY MANAGERS   GUILD MASTERS

Guild Masters

Global technology evangelist
SMEs and thought leaders

Focus:

- Technical vision and strategy
- Offer strategy and global
  coordination to communities
  within a guild

Community Managers

Managers and mentors, passionate
specialists in their technologies;
the scope is studio/countrywide

Focus:

- Talent leadership and development
- Capacity management: onboard and
  develop specialized talent to meet
  the business needs

Our Enterprise Software Guild Master, speaking at a Net meet-up in our Buenos Aires studio

Firefox

MOZILLA

Since its inception, Mozilla's mission has been to ensure the Internet is a global public resource, one that is open and accessible to all. Mozilla has always strived to put people first and help contribute to an Internet where individuals can shape their own experience and feel empowered, safe, and independent.

Mozilla's global community of technologists, thinkers, and builders work together to keep the Internet alive and approachable, enabling people worldwide to be informed creators of and contributors to the Web. This single-mindedness expanded with the launch of Firefox as an open-source browser, reaching new users from a mobile ecosystem.

Mozilla's commitment to human collaboration across an open platform is critical to individual growth and the collective future of the Internet.

Mitchell Baker,
Mozilla Executive
Chairwoman

"We were born as a radically open, radically participatory organization, unbound to traditional corporate structure. We played a role in bringing the 'open' movement into mainstream consciousness. Used thoughtfully, open practices can simultaneously build vibrant communities and provide competitive advantage."

Why It's Important

For talented individuals and groups to grow and realize their full potential, they need to be nurtured and supported.

Guilds, or skilled communities, of digital talent are valuable in that they help a company or organization embrace new technologies and practices, and can work on several tracks simultaneously. And a community goes beyond strictly functional roles, as it also **creates a feeling of belonging for community members.**

THE NEED FOR NURTURING YOUR PEOPLE

Help a company or organization embrace new technologies and practices, and work on several tracks simultaneously.

Community goes beyond strictly functional roles and creates a feeling of belonging.

Connecting talent to global communities builds a network of peers that support and learn from each other.

A SENSE OF BELONGING FOSTERS RETENTION

The purpose of a community is to create better professionals.

Communities can help develop and evolve skills, as well as career paths.

Strong communities attract talent in an age of scarcity.

Communities create thought leadership.

2

Benefits

A community's role is to nurture talent. A sense of belonging fosters retention of the best people. They rise to the top of their community, stay longer, and help attract others in an age where competition is fierce. The purpose of a community is to create better professionals while considering two dimensions: Execution and Consultancy. Execution comprises expertise and knowledge centered around design and engineering practices; consultancy implies understanding a customer's problem, developing and communicating an optimal solution. Communities can develop and evolve skills, and offer predictable career paths,which can lead to higher retention levels.

Keys to Success

COMMUNITIES MUST INSPIRE AND BUILD PRIDE

A strong community is where individuals can grow and diversify their talent

- Employees gain valuable skill sets in communities, which help reinforce loyalty and also keep them engaged with their new competencies.
- Keep community members inspired in smaller micro-ecosystems, while also ensuring and maintaining the traditional organizational management structure.

Connecting communities is more important than regulating their behavior

- Part of making that happen can be accomplished through roles that bring people and different communities together, rather than canceling what was already in place and working.

Communities must build a sense of belonging and pride

- That begins with individuals being proud to be associated with that community. Part of rootedness in the community requires establishing a leader to measure how it's performing and evolving.

An organic, proactive training process should be considered rather than one that's prescriptive

- This keeps a community current with the new skills, capabilities, and technologies shaping the market, thus avoiding being late to the next wave of change shaping the digital economy.

Motivating by recognizing merits and contributions

- A reward system should be established for incentivizing, coaching, and mentoring individuals who are seeking leadership roles before they are crowned leaders.

COMMUNITIES HELP FORGE UNIONS OF TRUST AND DRIVE THE VISION

Building community "circles of trust" allows businesses and partners to work in a more unified way.

A community's clear purpose and outcomes focus on the company's business needs and goals.

Communities can layer on top of the organization's existing functional areas and connect silos without creating turf-war friction.

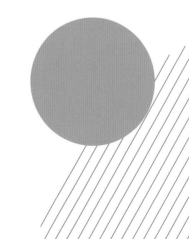

Reasons to Believe

Creating communities of talent helps forge unions of trust. By building these "circles of trust," businesses and their partners can work in a more unified manner, helping drive vision and opportunity for both organizations. Communities of talent are able to blend more easily into multidisciplinary pods, regardless of reporting structure.

When a community has clear purpose and understands its goals and objectives, it is more apt to leverage the passion of its talented people to help build bridges between internal employees and those who may work outside its traditional walls. This energy will often carry over when employees shift to different projects, build and design new technologies, and even move to new geographies.

Communities can extend beyond immediate responsibilities and job functions, and eventually help connect silos without creating turf wars or friction.

ENABLE SYSTEMIC TALENT GROWTH

The Industry Impact

At this phase, in what economists and analysts have labeled the Fourth Industrial Revolution, technology is evolving at a never-before-seen pace. This precedent requires a new way of thinking and embracing the most valuable assets in driving sustainable value: talented people. And most companies are in need of the skills and talent to help them transform their businesses.

Looking ahead, the global digital marketplace has a wealth of talent and skills to help companies build from on their path to digital transformation. Community members become the glue and catalysts that drive innovation and new initiatives that help establish new programs, products, and opportunities to pursue.

———

"Only 27% of **executives** have a cohesive digitization strategy across the enterprise."*

*Of 500 senior executives surveyed by Gartner

Embrace talent; they are the most valuable asset for driving value.

Community members become the glue and catalysts that drive innovation and new initiatives.

Partners' talent communities can spearhead your own community development program.

INSIDE THE DESIGN AND UX GUILD

—

An eight-step community recipe

1.

Define the scope of expertise and give names to your communities. Communities should consider what you are today and represent what you aspire your teams to become.

- ☑ **UX Director**
- ☑ **Interaction Designer**
- ☑ **UX Designer**
- ☑ **Visual Designer**
- ☑ **UX Researcher**
- ☑ **Illustrator**

2.

Identify core skills for each community and map them to your employees' profiles.

UX DESIGN

INTERACTIVE DESIGN

VISUAL   ILLUSTRATION

HTML RESEARCH

PHOTOSHOP **UI**

SKETCH

3.

Identify your community managers. You are looking for a technical person who is also passionate about people development.

Eugenio Calamari
Guild Master – UX & Design

Timeline   About   Followers

4.

Define the organizational model that works for you. If possible, make your teams report directly into communities. If this is too bold, make sure your community managers have a direct impact in community members' careers.

5.

Transition key people and career management processes to communities. Check if your performance management process is actually and constantly helping you build on top of your people's strengths.

7.

Create a communication plan and get professional help executing it … the internal audience is also worth spending your marketing dollars in!

6.

Select a collaboration platform and onboard your teams. Workplace, Microsoft Teams, Slack … whatever works for your organization and allows organic, peer-to-peer, formal, and informal collaboration.

8.

Define your KPIs to measure success of the model. Retention, engagement, growth, and thought leadership are some of the most valuable.

COMMUNITY MEMBERS CAN DEFINE THEIR CAREER PATHS, SIGNING UP FOR A DESTINATION COMMUNITY FOR TRAINING

PODIFY

—

Integrating Experience and
Talent Across the Enterprise

COMPANIES WITH TRADITIONAL ORGANIZATIONAL STRUCTURES CAN BEND AROUND THE CUSTOMER

To transform an organization, teams must be formed across silos and embrace a common operating model. Combined with the DNA of the tech partners' communities, pods are born.

BUILDING DREAM TEAMS

In order to transform an organization, teams must be formed to bring design and technology together in a natural way with a measurement-and-incentive system that drives behavior.

Spotify rose over several years to become a popular music provider widely known for delivering a broad selection of original music content. Analysts say that the start-up, launched in 2008, owed much of its success to its commitment to deeply rooted agile methodologies, which they call the Spotify Tribe. The Tribe is, not surprisingly, based on two core community values: autonomy and trust. Those qualities translate into realizing greater ownership and accountability for the work done. What's more, the Tribe was intentionally designed to create an environment where failure was taken as an opportunity to learn, innovate, and change. By doing so, it helped drive individual morale and growth for the company.

Pods provide companies and organizations with a cohesive way to design and build products.

Technology absent of design is neither compelling nor engaging.

Autonomy and trust are two core community values.

Spotify

In the late 1990s, Napster and peer-to-peer file-sharing services exploded onto the scene, and a debate raged regarding whether content should be free vs. what artists should be paid for their work. In some respects, Napster paved the way for Spotify, the music-streaming service that has been a successful but disruptive force, and actually pays royalties to musicians.

At last, music lovers had an easy-to-use and responsible platform to experience their favorite artists while also discovering new talent and genres. While users would search and find old and new hits, Spotify was collecting data and continually updating its engine. If you were a fan of the Killers, then Spotify's algorithm would make note and add it and similar music to your recommended playlist. By keeping track of what music you listen to, like, and skip over, Spotify continually curates a customized and personal mixtape exclusively for you.

Spotify's engineering culture is organized into agile, cross-functional teams across four different areas: squads, tribes, chapters, and guilds. Its approach to being agile has resulted in an autonomous structure, one that enables innovation without sacrificing accountability.

Culture plays a big role in keeping the innovation engine firing on all cylinders. Spotify has an experiment-friendly culture with an emphasis on test-and-learn approaches and contained experiments. If people don't know the best way to do something, they are likely to try alternative approaches and run several A/B tests to determine which is preferable. Spotify's approach uses data and experimentation to support an open dialogue about root causes.

PRODUCT, DESIGN, ENGINEERING, AND QUALITY ASSURANCE COMMUNITIES DON'T OFTEN SYNERGIZE STANDING ALONE

—

Delivering sustainable business outcomes.

—

Combining disciplines from different communities.

—

Reinforcing values for clients: quality, efficiency, and predictability.

Why It's Important

Companies are often siloed so that product, design, engineering, and quality assurance organizations are separate and don't work together effectively. In short, product and design teams throw requirements "over the wall" and start asking engineering when the product will be delivered.

Pods are the answer to bridging these divides from small- to large-scale projects and partners. Pods are dedicated agile teams that deliver sustainable innovation and results. They combine disciplines from different communities to help build custom products and innovative solutions.

What is a pod? Pods are cross-functional, agile teams, ideally sized eight to ten people, responsible for end-to-end solutions and focused on meeting business objectives.

Pods operate within the pod model, which combines any agile development framework of choice with a methodology that surfaces best practices and performance in the shape of key performance indicators, or KPIs, aligned with strategic goals.

The pod methodology can be tailored to any partner and promotes effective delivery and sustainability in three main ways:

- By breaking down traditional functional silos
- By maintaining a lean and solid process
- By measuring value delivered to the business and, ultimately, success

Functional silos are no longer relevant — even individual performance loses significance — as the focus shifts to team or pod results. How does this team self-organize in order to meet their objectives? What are the outcomes expected from this team, and how will their performance be measured?

For a team to perform at its best, a few things need to happen:

1) **Strategic goals:** shared alignment of business goals, or what we call strategic goals. This is understood and shared across all members of the pod and all related pods.
2) **Cross-functionality:** the right pod composition nurtured by the communities coming together in the pod and working toward that strategic goal.
3) **Tracking:** measuring what matters, paving the way, and shedding light on the road toward that strategic goal. This is why simply measuring velocity and quality is not enough. We structure our KPIs in four dimensions: Velocity, Quality, Product Impact, and Autonomy. The selected KPIs will be specific to the project, its strategic goal, and moment in time.

Partners, and by extension, clients, value quality, efficiency, and predictability. Pods help deliver all of these benefits while also helping build a relationship of trust and open communication. The pod model also allows businesses to shape behavior by creating alignment at the outset with the client's standards (What Good Looks Like — WGLL) and defining meaningful KPIs jointly between the pod and the internal and external client. Transformational partnerships will closely monitor the results of these KPIs to hone the performance of a pod or many pods.

HOW ARE PODS CONFIGURED?

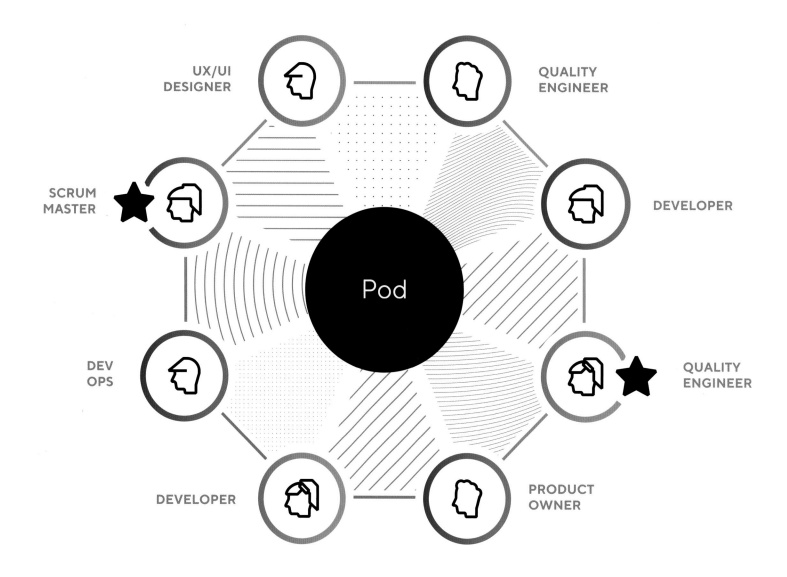

UX/UI DESIGNER

QUALITY ENGINEER

SCRUM MASTER

DEVELOPER

DEV OPS

Pod

QUALITY ENGINEER

DEVELOPER

PRODUCT OWNER

Core members are SMEs (subject matter experts) that have the technical, leadership, and communication skills to drive a team toward success.

Core members know what good looks like and are highly valued by both the team and the stakeholders. There is a path to becoming a core member, and this career path within a pod must be agreed upon by the partners.

MEASURING WHAT MATTERS

Pod results are data-driven and measured in four dimensions:

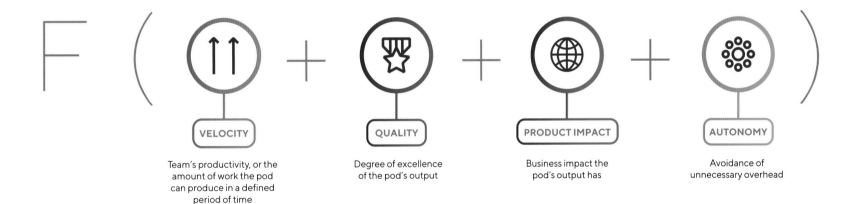

$$F\left(\text{VELOCITY} + \text{QUALITY} + \text{PRODUCT IMPACT} + \text{AUTONOMY} \right)$$

VELOCITY
Team's productivity, or the amount of work the pod can produce in a defined period of time

QUALITY
Degree of excellence of the pod's output

PRODUCT IMPACT
Business impact the pod's output has

AUTONOMY
Avoidance of unnecessary overhead

Pods are purpose-built, cross-functional delivery teams.

Pods focus on products and solutions, and are fueled by communities.

Specific KPIs within each dimension are unique to each pod.

Benefits

Pods have all of the skills to wholly own and deliver digital products. They provide companies and organizations with a cohesive working group to design and build products that require a high degree of design and technology competencies.

In doing so, the pods become the nucleus of digital partnerships, helping nourish, grow, and evolve skills and talents. Pods help create and sustain consistency and "stickiness," whereby teams and partners build greater trust and competency. When it comes to creating evolutionary prototypes, pods are extremely valuable in that they allow teams to evolve the products as they embrace innovative trends and technologies.

Pods become the intersection of insights and action, where these two forces combine to provide an incremental path for development. Because of their synergistic focus with multidisciplinary teams as pod ecosystem grows, a culture forms where an agile mindset, product, and results are at the center of the value system.

PODS BLEND DIVERSE TALENTS FROM COMMUNITIES AND ACHIEVE BUSINESS OUTCOMES

Pods are the nucleus of digital partnerships, helping to create and sustain consistency, eventually becoming the focal point of insights and action.

CONNECTING DIFFERENT FUNCTIONAL GROUPS WITHIN THE BUSINESS DRIVES OWNERSHIP AND DELIVERY

Don't fall into the trap of isolated agile coaching programs. Transform at scale through pods as change agents.

Use pods to break silos

- The pod framework connects different functional groups within the business so that a single team can own the delivery of a digital product. One of the key points is connecting product visionaries and designers with the engineering teams to enable flexibility and agility. What's more, these interactions help set into motion an evolutionary path for each pod in which good practices pay off.

Focus on agile best practices and define WGLL

- Iterate and improve leveraging KPIs to track your maturity path. Use KPIs strategically to communicate clearly: wins, red flags, deviations, and root causes.
- Have objective conversations, and get accountable parties to commit to tactical improvement plans.

Elicit and show quick wins

- Identify and leverage core members from your and neighboring pods, appreciating wins and learning from them to propel your pod's growth. Align toward the business's strategic goals, identifying the KPIs that will track your journey and the pod's value-add. Measure the pod's output and take tactical action.

Pods to drive change

- With room to breathe, pods become change agents. A pod with 20% velocity improvement will not only affect change within the team, but it will also help inspire and mobilize change in the surrounding environment. This is transformative change in action and at scale; these micro-changes help create high-performance environments.

WHAT TO MEASURE
HOW TO STRATEGICALLY SELECT YOUR KPIs?

What is your business goal?

- What is value-add?
- What problem are you trying to solve?
- Are there friction points?
- What are the project's main risks?

Define KPIs

- Define KPIs for each dimension: Velocity, Quality, Product Impact, and Autonomy.
- Assign weight to each dimension based on value-add definition.
- Identify the purpose for each KPI within the four dimensions.

Use KPIs strategically

- KPIs should mark your pod's successes.
- KPIs should raise red flags on achievements of time to allow for course correction.
- KPIs should enable continuous improvement to eliminate friction points.
- KPIs should render subjective conversations objective.

Already tracking KPIs?

- Make sure you cover all four dimensions: Velocity, Quality, Product Impact, and Autonomy.
- Give them strategic focus.
- Analyze trends and variations and all KPIs in relationship to one another.
- Tell your story: share your interpretation with your stakeholders.
- Define your pod's maturity path.

Define your maturity path

- Match the pod's capabilities with the organization's strategic goals.
- For each KPI, have the pod define various targets — Level 1, 2, etc. — to reach a proposed timeline.
- Monitor, review, communicate, and adjust as needed.

Target your audience

- Differentiate KPIs for tactical management vs. strategic tracking.
- Don't focus solely on numbers: observe and analyze trends.
- Control the message: interpret, analyze, and communicate your KPIs.

Adjust systems, processes, and environments to leap forward

- Maturity path is set for the pod.

PODS BECOME AN INTEGRAL ENGINE WHERE VARIOUS TALENTS AND SKILL SETS COMBINE FORCES

Reasons to Believe

Pods are the meeting grounds where digital partners can safely experiment in a cohesive way and forge a path to achieve their goals. They also depend on each other for assets, components, and information. This collective strength, derived from a pod network effect, can help combine various company capabilities yet not be encumbered by common divisional or political boundaries. As an ecosystem, individual pods can have the same top-level goals, which means that sharing extends across all pods in a business or organization. The genius of the pod is that it focuses on collective power, has clear objectives and shared KPIs (which improve the product), and melts away many of these protective urges. With clear goals and KPIs working in conjunction, the pod takes on a dynamic where it evolves and continues to grow and outperform itself by delivering benefits to the project or development effort.

Pods blend skills from diverse communities, as a least-disruptive way to collapse silos.

The genius of the pod is the collective power aligned with a group objective.

BEING DIGITAL IS NOT ELECTIVE SURGERY

The Industry Impact

According to Forrester, "in 2019, digital transformation moves from super-wide enterprise efforts to a pragmatic, surgical portfolio view of digital investments with the goal of making incremental and necessary changes to operations. In fact, 25% of firms will decelerate digital efforts altogether and lose market share."

Looking ahead, **pods are essential vehicles for companies to conceive, design, and build new products in this new digital-transformation era.** The traditional software development paradigm is less flexible in how it defines, builds, and tests software projects. In today's highly dynamic and complex digital landscape, large and small companies need to adjust to these dynamic dimensions.

As new kinds of technologies come into play, such as AI and machine learning, prototypes can be created so teams can continue to grow with the surrounding array of complex technologies and infrastructure. **Both pods and the surrounding ecosystem are agile and very adaptable to change.**

"In 2018, more than **50% of digital transformation** efforts stalled."

According to Forrester: "Predictions 2019: Transformation Goes Pragmatic"

THE POD MODEL

Pods

Pods combine talent from guilds dedicated to partners. The core DNA of the pods intersects digital expertise and intimate knowledge of the business.

- Cross-functional agile teams
- Ideal size: eight to ten people
- Autonomous and responsible for end-to-end solutions
- Focused on meeting client's objectives

Pod Framework

The pods methodology is tailored to each partner and promotes effective delivery and sustainability by:

- Keeping a lean and solid process
- Measuring KPI-driven performance
- Providing the ability to easily scale without impacting the team performance

Development Framework

The development framework will be defined with the client and should preferably be an agile framework. Scrum and Kanban are the most frequently used.

Game of Pods

The gamification process integrates pods and communities and helps model behavior with a motivation, bottom-up, empowering approach, by rewarding both collective and individual contribution.

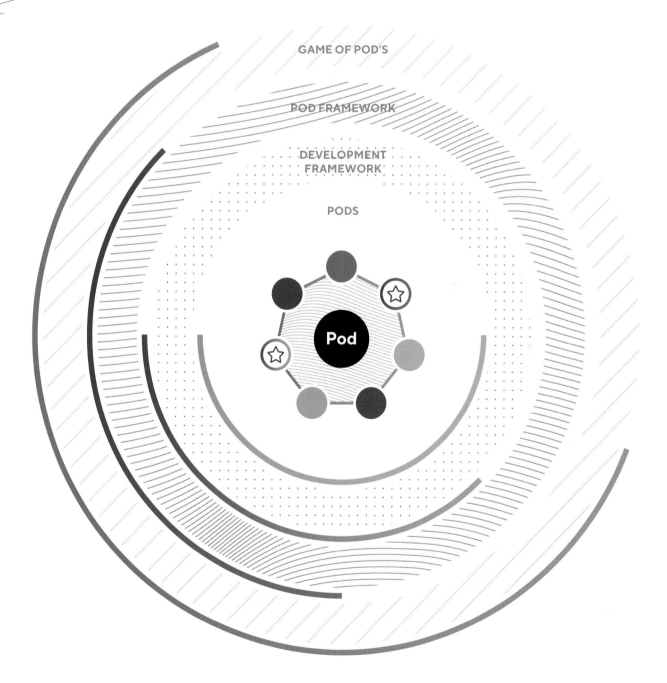

GAME OF POD'S

POD FRAMEWORK

DEVELOPMENT
FRAMEWORK

PODS

Pod

A CULTURE OF CONTINUOUS IMPROVEMENT

———

Motivation by Design

RECOGNIZING MERITS AND CONTRIBUTIONS

Create a platform that will inspire new and sustainable behavior.

The next generations of digital natives do not embrace, process, or feel motivation from instruction. They need a support platform that marries their personal contributions and results they achieve working within pods to their career paths. This new generation of digital natives see the world through a more meritocratic lens.

They do not appreciate political moves without merit, they view their contributions as a way to advance their careers, and they are always hungry for recognition. They have grown up in an environment of high exposure and social tension, where opinions aggregate and converge organically through social networks, where the clout of traditional leadership often collapses under the scrutiny of the masses. All this tension is relieved in environments where "play" connects, rewards, and trains. In the work environment, and particularly within partnerships with a strong focus on transformational results, barriers of entry for people and teams should be low. This means individuals and teams that contribute, support,

and create micro-improvements should be visible, recognized, and celebrated. Their careers should improve as they produce these changes in an environment where fairness prevails. Intrinsic motivation works at play.

You will require new behaviors from your teams as your business evolves and adapts to new markets and disruptive technologies. How do you drive behavior from your teams to be ahead of the game? For this new generation of workers, it's definitely not by policing or by implementing old-school rewards systems. Rather, it's by incentivizing a growth mindset where individuals within a community improve themselves and the environment around them.

Game of Pods is a platform and a methodology that embraces our nature, meets the needs of a generation that grew up in the digital era playing games, and welcomes the need to accelerate the progression toward highly effective outcome-driven teams at work.

DIGITAL NATIVES WANT TO MARRY THEIR PERSONAL CONTRIBUTIONS AND RESULTS TO SHORT-TERM RECOGNITION AND LONG-TERM CAREER GROWTH

—

Individuals and teams that contribute, support, and create micro-improvements should be visible, recognized, and celebrated.

—

It allows pods and clients to track progress and act as a vehicle to socialize, motivate, and viralize behavior with support from above but driven by each pod.

—

Incentivize a growth mindset where individuals within a community improve themselves and the environment around them.

GAME OF PODS

Game of Pods is the gamification of the delivery process that integrates pods and communities to drive a culture of developing applications using pod-development methodologies and modern engineering principles. It focuses on both individual and collective contributions.

The first is done with a 360-degree approach where peers and managers are awarding personal recognitions based on day-to-day interactions with the individual. The second is all about the pod, and what a group of individuals can achieve when they come together following the pod philosophy. The focus is on the output of the pod, and the approach fully empowers the pod to map out its own journey through Game of Pods based on best applying practices. The pod is setting goals and targets and collecting badges and trophies, the sum of which will define it's maturity level.

It allows partners to track the progress of the pod's maturity path and acts as a vehicle to socialize, motivate, and viralize behavior with support from above but driven by each pod. **"Driven from below, shared across, and supported from above" is the motto for Game of Pods.**

1. Earn Personal Badges

Focus on individual contribution above and beyond daily project activities.

- Personal growth
  (certification, training, domain knowledge)
- Community contribution
  (interviews, thought leadership, mentoring)
- Peer-to-peer recognition
  (aligned with corporate values)

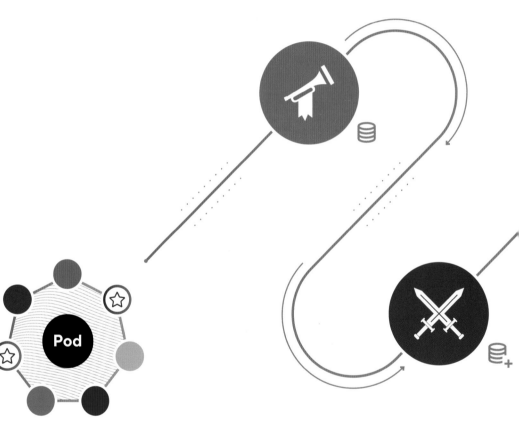

2. Earn Pod Badges

Focus on collective contributions.

- Health of the project
- Performance of the pod
- Quality of the delivery
- Achievement of product KPIs

3. Earn Pod Trophies

Reaching milestones based
on pod's output.

- Measurable value delivered (KPIs)
- Growth
- Stakeholder satisfaction

5. Celebrate!

Keep your team motivated.
Celebrate small and big wins.

- Team celebrations
- Workplace leaderboards
- Social sharing
- Tech meet-ups

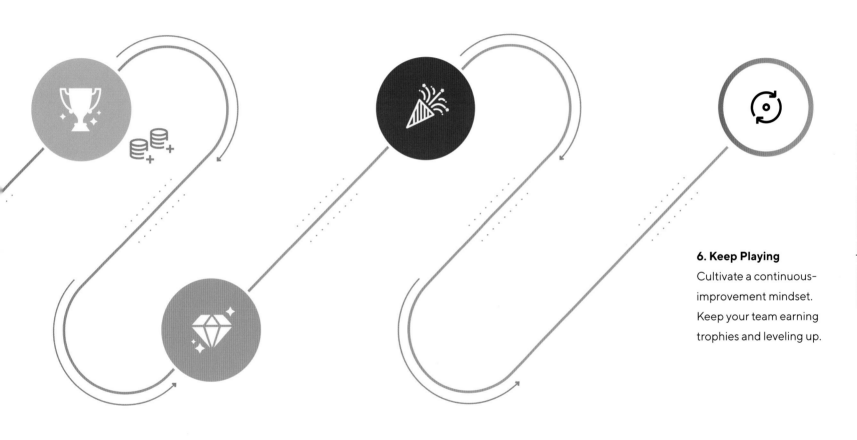

6. Keep Playing

Cultivate a continuous-
improvement mindset.
Keep your team earning
trophies and leveling up.

4. Level Up Your Pod

Pod's maturity is determined by
the sum of badges and trophies.

- Rookie
- Amateur
- Proficient
- Advanced
- Expert

MOTIVATING WITH EMPOWERMENT

Why It's Important

Game of Pods inspires and measures team performance and delivery, fostering best practices and collaboration while also encouraging and monitoring individual performance. The global gamification program is designed to provide timely and superior value to the partnership by empowering teams to tailor what superior service looks like to the specific needs of their stakeholders. In Game of Pods, individuals are recognized for their contributions above and beyond the expectations of the project, such as personal growth and contributions to the community.

This initiative recognizes efforts that usually go unnoticed, and brings to the forefront the culture of continuous improvement at a personal level, helping build communities from the bottom up.

In parallel, the pods are earning badges and trophies following a maturity path that they themselves have defined — and continuously validate and iterate — together with their business counterparts. The actions the pod takes toward improving its output are monitored to ensure project health, quality of delivery, high performance of the pod, and full alignment with their product or business outcome goals. As the

pod transitions its maturity path, it is recognized for proving its increased maturity through measurable value delivered, ability to scale both in size and cross-functionality, and customer satisfaction.

It's a fun way to motivate, and in doing so, it shapes and models behavior. As it is a social tool, recognitions are celebrated and shared with all employees. Game of Pods is the epitome of gamification in action and enables companies to reach a higher level of efficiency and professionalism while challenging employees to achieve personal goals in a fun, team-oriented process. Additional upsides include:

- A flexible model that can work in any environment, laying on top of any development framework and practices chosen by the pod and the pod's stakeholders (business partners, product owners, leadership, etc.).
- The embodiment of team empowerment, incentivizing pods and individuals to be and continuously strive for better.
- An approach that encourages diverse thinking that recognizes teams and individuals for their value-add, as opposed to simply adhering to rules.

Simplifying and improving
learning and sharing

Boosting people's morale

Increasing engagement

India Studio: Diversity of thinking is a hallmark.

Meritocracy is a system of allocating rewards via competitions and incentive structures, underpinned by a principle of equality. In a sense, meritocracy ensures that people deserve the outcomes that they get.

Benefits

Game of Pods enables a company to reach a higher level of efficiency and professionalism, and allows its employees to challenge themselves and achieve their personal goals while at the same time achieving organizational goals. In doing so, it also becomes a vehicle to socialize, motivate, and viralize a different way of working that leverages networks instead of fixed structures. Several benefits fall under the headings of the following three categories:

Organizationally: It promotes best practices and behaviors by empowering individuals and pods to earn badges and trophies, resulting in pods outperforming themselves iteratively and inducing a continuous push for excellence.

Motivationally: It creates a healthy, competitive culture that showcases pods who are adhering to the pod's principles and highlights individuals who are actively supporting their community, while providing coaching opportunities for those who are not.

Competitively: It empowers teams with a bottom-up/pull mechanism that incentivizes all pod members to collaborate and maximize their potential to produce business value through a distinct KPI framework shared with the stakeholders, acting as a clear differentiator from competitors.

When Game of Pods is working, it becomes infectious and addictive, just like a game. The system catches on naturally. It's a positive-reinforcement system that perfectly aligns incentives with desired outcomes.

A SYSTEMATIC AND FUN WAY TO RAISE MERITOCRACY

 Game of Pods allows its employees to challenge themselves and achieve their personal goals.

 Game of Pods is the epitome of gamification in action and enables companies to reach a higher level of efficiency and professionalism.

 The game becomes a vehicle to socialize, motivate, and viralize a different way of working that leverages networks.

REWARD COLLECTIVE AND INDIVIDUAL CONTRIBUTIONS

—

By rewarding both collective and individual contributions, Game of Pods integrates pods and communities in a way that helps model behavior and values toward a meritocratic culture. In essence, it provides a motivating, bottom-up, empowering approach. Ultimately, it is designed to provide timely and better results.

1

Define your strategic goals

- What are the business goals you are trying to achieve?

Break down your goals into actionable items

- These are the specific behaviors that will lead you to achieve your delivery goals. For example: project KPIs, agile development practices, innovation, client alignment, cross functionality, and product focus.

Game on!

Constantly reassess:
- Are business outcomes being met?
- What are the pod KPI trends?
- Are there changes in the context to effect better results?
- Are you getting the desired behaviors?
- Are the reward systems compatible?

Tailor the game to your desired outcomes

- Define who your participants are and the type of behavior you want to model in your teams. Design your recognitions system: badges, trophies, experience points, and progression levels. You may also want to consider monetary rewards, but make sure you don't confuse them or override the intrinsic motivation your players get from progressing in the game.

Implement your game MVP

- Chose the platform on which the game will be played. The right platform has to be familiar and accessible to all participants, not a barrier of entry. Start small, leveraging your current tool set, and build incrementally as you get feedback from early engagement. Make it data-driven, using analytics to track performance and to adjust recognitions in order to incentivize the right behaviors.

Game of Pods integrates pods and communities to drive a culture of continuous improvement.

Pods become vehicles to socialize, motivate, and viralize behavior.

Reasons to Believe

With a gamification process that links pods and communities, companies can better monitor the progress of each pod on its maturity path. The pod becomes a vehicle to socialize, motivate, and viralize behavior with support from leadership, but driven by each pod. This approach translates into scalability and sustainability, activating an engine that encourages and infuses continuous improvement across the ecosystem. It motivates and generates a culture of doers that feel empowered by an environment of trust and accountability to take action toward growth, and that mentality is recognized both at a team and individual levels.

POD MATURITY LEADS TO HIGH PERFORMANCE

THE BEST PLAYERS DON'T MAKE THE BEST TEAM IF THEY ARE NOT ENGAGED

The Industry Impact

Companies have begun to realize the benefits of game mechanics as a method to structure human behavior that encourages innovation, productivity, and engagement.

Still, the idea of motivating and growing talent has been an age-old challenge for every company and organization in just about every work era. This is particularly true today in terms of recruiting millennials. Author Chris Tuff's book, entitled *The Millennial Whisperer,* offers strategies for success as well as advice on hiring and retaining millennials.

Three strategies for success from *The Millennial Whisperer* include:

- **Serve their needs:** Millennials need purpose and want acknowledgment and to profit not just financially, but also with social capital.
- **Create structure:** Millennials need a structured work environment that inspires and provides autonomy.
- **Invest in culture:** Millennials want a culture that is diverse, serves the community, and is socially connected.

In addition, advice for recognizing millennials runs deeper than just a raise or a bonus. Instead of looking at a financial bottom line, choose a more personal approach, like concert tickets or a gift card to a favorite restaurant. And last, respect and help them make time for passion projects such as charities, volunteerism, and travel.

These personal approaches to recognition will help reward and retain talent in an authentic, lasting manner.

Gamification encourages innovation, productivity, and engagement.

Gallup indicates that 70% of all business leaders believe employee engagement is critical to their organization's success while only 13% of global employees working for an organization are engaged.*

* involved in, enthusiastic about, and committed to their work and workplace

INSIDE THE GAME OF PODS

An Example

Two Pods in the Game

Two new pods are brought on board to help our stakeholders develop their new SAAS application.

They have a tight timeline and are working with both in-house and partner teams. Each pod is meant to be a cross-functional team, ideally of eight to ten members, which works autonomously on implementing an end-to-end solution to meet the client's objectives.

The teams are assembled, and the group is invited to define their own identity as a result of their own creative teamwork. They define their name, avatar, and mission statement. It's a fun activity that will help the team members get to know each other as well as ensure the understanding of the common goal.

Deactivate hero culture by infusing a sense of purpose in the pod.

PODS NEED AN IDENTITY:
DEFINE NAME, AVATAR, AND MISSION

THE TRANSFORMERS POD

We transform beyond the boundaries of the digital; resistance is futile.

THE RAVEN POD

A raven's perspective is to find smart solutions where human beings fail. When solutions are not on the earth, a raven will fly to develop amazing and magical code.

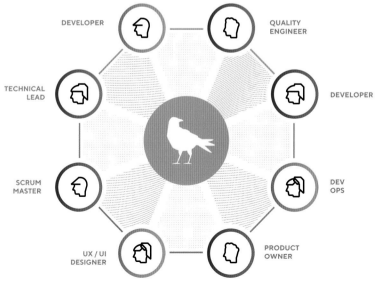

DESIGNING PODS' MATURITY PATH

The pods will adopt an agile framework. The pod framework urges them to build business and practice KPIs and create a maturity path that defines the evolution and success of the pod over time and focuses on achieving business outcomes.

SCRUM	BEST PRACTICES	KPIS
2-WEEK SPRINTS WITH: • SPRINT PLANNING • GROOMING • STANDUPS • DEMO • RETROSPECTIVE	• CODE REVIEWS • DONE CRITERIA WITH PRODUCT SIGN-OFF • UNIT TESTING 60%	**BURNDOWN CHART:** • VELOCITY (# OF STORY POINTS PER SPRINT) • ESCAPED DEFECTS (# OF BUGS EXPERIENCED BY USERS IN PRODUCTION) • CODE COVERAGE (% OF CODE COVERED BY UNIT TEST)

DIMENSIONS	WEIGHT	CRITERIA	METRIC	TARGET			REVIEW
				LEVEL 1	LEVEL 2	LEVEL 3	
	40%	PRODUCTIVITY	# OF STORY POINTS COMPLETED	102 SP	122 SP	140 SP	PER SPRINT
		PREDICTABILITY	SAY/DO RADIO	90%	95%	98%	PER SPRINT
		RESPONSIVENESS	CYCLE TIME	TBD	TBD	TBD	PER SPRINT
	20%	OUTPUT	# OF DEFECTS	< 20	< 13	< 8	PER SPRINT
			# OF ESCAPED DEFECTS	0	0	0	PER RELEASE
			% OF UNIT TEST COVERAGE	60%	75%	90%	PER RELEASE
	25%	PRODUCT	COMPLETED PBI ACCEPTED RATIO	95%	98%	100%	PER SPRINT
			BACKLOG HEALTH INDEX	200 SP P1&P2	250 SP P1&P2	300 SP P1&P2	PER SPRINT
		BUSINESS	APP ADOPTION	20%	25%	30%	PER RELEASE
	15%	TECHNICAL MASTERY	CORE MEMBERS PER POD	30%	35%	40%	PER QUARTER
		ADAPTABILITY	# OF PROCESS IMPROVEMENTS	3	5	8	PER QUARTER

VELOCITY   **QUALITY**   **PRODUCT IMPACT**   **AUTONOMY**

CREATING AN INVENTORY OF AWARDS

Pod Badges

☑ Set up your KPIs

☑ Applied development best practices

☑ Applied project-management best practices

☑ Aligned with your client

☑ Set up an effective governance model

☑ Applied a design system

☑ Added additional skills to pod

Trophies

☑ Exceeded your target KPIs

☑ Filled partners' skills or experience deficiencies

☑ Spun off new pods

☑ Surpassed customer expectations

Level Up Your Pod

☑ Combined badges and trophies to level up

☑ Defined the maturity path — which KPIs to improve, how much, and by when

☑ Defined target KPIs for Level 1 through 4, and tracked pod's maturity path

☑ Started pod as a Rookie and earned trophies to level up through Amateur, Proficient, Advanced, and Expert

The value is not in the individual badge, but in the collective contribution. The team builds its unique configuration, much like a beehive.

Agile
Development
Practices

KPIs

Cross-disciplines =
path to proficiency

THE TRANSFORMERS POD JOURNEY

SPRINT 0	SPRINT 1	SPRINT 2	SPRINT 3	SPRINT 4
				200 XP
POD LEVEL ROOKIE	30 XP	50 XP	90 XP	

Pod reviews existing KPIs and applies them within the pod model to identify gaps			Team has baselined and defines maturity path	Adds an Architect to the pod Adopts TDD

	Badge for practicing Scrum with all its ceremonies Badge for cross-functionality Badge for DevOps capabilities within the pod	Badge for having a product and design working with engineering in one pod Badge for basic level of unit test coverage	Badges for defining Velocity, Quality, Product Impact, and Autonomy KPIs	Badge for having an Architect in the pod Trophy for cross-functionality: having 5+ communities within a pod

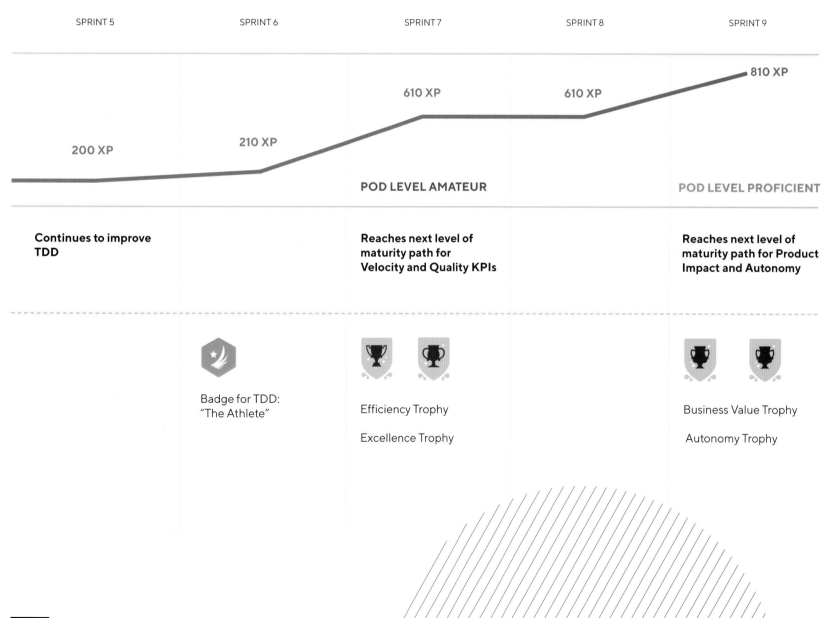

SPRINT 5   SPRINT 6   SPRINT 7   SPRINT 8   SPRINT 9

810 XP

610 XP   610 XP

200 XP   210 XP

POD LEVEL AMATEUR   **POD LEVEL PROFICIENT**

Continues to improve TDD

Reaches next level of maturity path for Velocity and Quality KPIs

Reaches next level of maturity path for Product Impact and Autonomy

Badge for TDD: "The Athlete"

Efficiency Trophy

Excellence Trophy

Business Value Trophy

Autonomy Trophy

THE RAVEN POD JOURNEY

SPRINT 0	SPRINT 1	SPRINT 2	SPRINT 3	SPRINT 4
	30 XP	40 XP	80 XP	190 XP

POD LEVEL ROOKIE

Pod reviews existing KPIs and applies them within the pod model to identify gaps

Team has baselined and defines maturity path

Adds an Architect to the pod

Badge for practicing Scrum with all its ceremonies

Badge for cross-functionality

Badge for DevOps capabilities within the pod

Badge for having a product and design working with engineering in one pod

Badges for defining Velocity, Quality, Product Impact, and Autonomy KPIs

Badge for having an Architect in the pod

Trophy for cross-functionality: having 5+ communities within a pod

	SPRINT 5	SPRINT 6	SPRINT 7	SPRINT 8	SPRINT 9
	200 XP	200 XP	400 XP	600 XP	600 XP

POD LEVEL AMATEUR

Improves the level of communication, reporting, and risk management	Reaches next level of maturity path for Autonomy	Reaches next level of maturity path for Quality

Badge for reporting and risk management: "The Mitigator"

Autonomy Trophy

Excellence Trophy

DESIGN IS HOW IT WORKS*

* Steve Jobs

EXPERIENCES ARE ENABLED BY DESIGN

Good Experiences

Lead to Engagement

REALIZING WHAT MATTERS

Digital Services That Drive Engagement Can Transform Industries

"Design thinking" is a collection of methods and tools that help solve problems and can be employed across the spectrum of business operations.

We live and work in an exciting time where digital products and services are transforming industries, business models, and jobs. Whether it is the uberization of everything from home automation to personalized medicine, or the blurring boundaries of digital and physical channels, businesses and industries are going through a period of mass disruption. This transformation continues to accelerate, placing more pressure on companies and brands to stay ahead, which involves the dual challenge of maintaining both their customer's loyalty and their attention. At the same time, consumers and employees are becoming overwhelmed with the digital proliferation of channels, devices, touch points, and tools.

Stitch Fix is an online fashion retailer that sends a woman named Selina clothing choices based on her preferences, behavioral data, available inventory, trends, and its own style curation algorithm. Selina values the recommendations and service because they are personal but also seem spontaneous. This surprises and delights her.

The boundaries have blurred between digital and physical as technologies such as IoT have helped objects, devices, and machines get "smart." This convergence has meant businesses can no longer afford to operate in segregated silos, such as production, sales, marketing, and IT.

A design-led business openly embraces the idea of continuous change, which is part of today's digital marketplace demands.

Today, the focus and mindset zeroes in on how a company can impact and improve customers' lives, such as what Airbnb and Uber have done for us. This contrasts past approaches, where companies had a clearly defined product focused on profitability.

Uber and Uber Eats are good examples for how companies are leveraging a core competency to not just grow their business, but also build their reputation and demand among core audiences. While Uber helped usher in the era of car-sharing, it is aggregating its service to build a bridge to its customer, and offering an integrated experience.

Now, instead of just a ride from Uber, you can get meals or groceries delivered straight to your door. Uber has leveraged and aggregated its design to explore new revenue streams, while continuing to deliver on customer service and experience across all channels.

In 2011, disruption arrived in a big way at the doorstep of the fashion retail industry. Stitch Fix changed shopping experiences and expectations forever by offering 'picked-by-a-stylist' apparel and accessories. The online styling subscription service features input from customers, along with collaboration between human stylists and AI. This unique combination has empowered a growing user base, delivering regularly scheduled and personalized recommendations, while eliminating painful trips to crowded shopping malls and time wasted with online shopping.

The service is ideal for customers pressed for time or looking to add new and different pieces to their wardrobe. Customers keep what they want and return what they don't like. Central to its model, all this information and feedback is captured by the company, ultimately improving individual algorithms to better determine each person's preferred style.

The company began with one machine-learning algorithm. Today, Stitch Fix has hundreds collecting and analyzing data. The more collaboration that happens between Stitch Fix humans and machines, the more efficiencies the business realizes. Over time, Stitch Fix learns more about what customers want, which cuts down on returns as well as warehouse space.

Katrina Lake,
CEO of Stitch Fix

Stitch Fix

"Other apparel retailers attempt to differentiate themselves through the lowest price or the fastest shipping; we differentiate ourselves through personalization. One-hundred percent of our revenue results directly from our recommendations, which are the core of our business."

DISCOVERING THE WHY CAN LEAD TO STRONG CONVERSION

Why It's Important

Design-driven companies do more than just deliver goods and services for what customers want: they understand and uncover the rationale. It's just as important to them to understand why they want it. Getting to the why is not always easy, and data alone is not the answer, because it does not often reveal sentiment. Design-driven companies invest a great deal of time observing, listening, and learning the motivation behind why and how people experience and use their products. Motivation could be based on being disruptive, or surprising and delighting with a unique experience. There are opportunities for creating moments that will help a person experience a product differently on their decision journey.

Design-led businesses
embrace continuous change.

Strong engagement is fueled
by design thinking.

A design studio becomes ground zero for discovery and innovation.

Benefits

Good design inspires and advances culture, collaboration, and communities. Razor-sharp design strategy can address a variety of business challenges, including retention and sales, while encouraging and inspiring the sales force to innovate and develop new strategies and ideas that will lead to tangible business results company-wide.

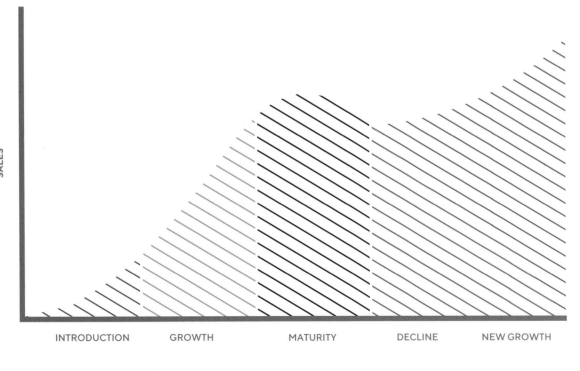

SALES

RE-IMAGINED
EXPERIENCE

SALES

INTRODUCTION   GROWTH   MATURITY   DECLINE   NEW GROWTH

TIME

EMBEDDED DESIGN GIVES LIFE AND EXTENDS THE PRODUCT LIFE CYCLE

KNOW AND UNDERSTAND YOUR CUSTOMERS' DIGITAL FRICTION POINTS

Design the service

- Let the design process reveal challenges and opportunities throughout the business.
- Look at process, operations, and your resources as adaptable elements.
- Know your customer and the market and design new business models. Become indispensable to your customers.

Create flexible design frameworks

2

- Develop and embrace design systems that are scalable and build consensus.
- Focus on interactivity that contributes to the broader experience.
- Work toward a reduction in time to market.

4

Build cocreation spaces

- Thinking outside the box also implies thinking outside your everyday space.
- Studios enable collaboration that fosters deep integration, alignment, and rapid outcomes.
- Consider setting up a dedicated design studio, either yourself or through your partners.

3

Adapt product design for an agile mindset

- As markets change, businesses need to pivot.
- Agile empowers and enables companies to be more productive, delivering higher quality products and engagement.
- Companies are better positioned for success and to deliver value when design systems are fully integrated.

A SPACE FOR CO-CREATION: THE STUDIO

For centuries, artists have sought the refuge of a studio to hone their skills and innovate. It is a place where inspiration and expertise mix, encouraging something more than the sum of the parts. In many ways, a studio becomes ground zero for discovery, sharing, and innovation due to the synergistic gathering of multidisciplinary abilities and talents that help expand the realm of what's possible.

Studios are focused R&D labs that create the capacity and capabilities that scale innovation. Members of the studio play with cutting-edge ideas and technologies. In a studio, members form a community which opens up and forges new bonds, thereby creating new possibilities through the collective imagination and purpose of the group.

There are several examples of companies that have made significant investments in designing workplaces that encourage collaboration and inspiration. Amazon, Apple, and Google all have headquarters that bring people together to bond and innovate. Open studios and design spaces encourage physical activity and results in employees who are more alert and ultimately more insightful. Google was an early pioneer in promoting movement in its office, building a large rock-climbing wall within its NYC headquarters. It also offers a variety of workspace options, including beanbag chairs and swing sets. This campus-like setting itself is a community, advancing team-building and knowledge-sharing. This movement and bringing together of people helps foster cocreation, even at a global level.

Studios are able to accomplish, on a small scale, the innovation cultivation that is essential for a balanced and thriving performance ecosystem.

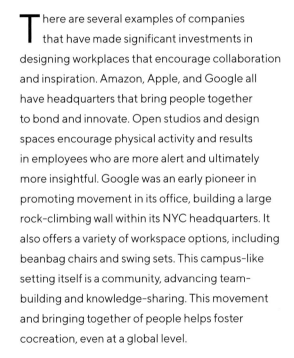

Reasons to Believe

A great example and proof point for how effective design processes and thinking can be is Netflix, which has been wildly successful at recommending shows to people based on past viewership and history. Given its successful combination of human selection and automation, and the fact it pays particularly close attention to viewers' personal preferences with respect to streaming, Netflix revenue has been growing more than 30% on an annualized basis.

Netflix's approach to design process and thinking has enabled customers to take advantage of intelligent and intuitive interfaces that power a personalized experience, and this has led to customer acquisition, satisfaction, and growth.

Customer-obsessed companies that embrace design financially outperform their peers.

The user should be at the heart of the strategic decision process.

Design becomes the fuel to drive innovation and helps inspire meaningful strategies.

By embracing design processes, a company places the user at the heart of strategic decision-making and helps frame an evidence-based business strategy.

DMI and Motiv Strategies, funded by Microsoft, began analyzing the performance of US companies committed to design as an integral part of their business strategy. Completed in 2013, the Design Value Index tracked the value of publicly held companies that met specific design management criteria, and monitored the impact of their investments in design on stock value over a ten-year period relative to the overall S&P Index.

ACCELERATING
AGILE PRODUCT DESIGN

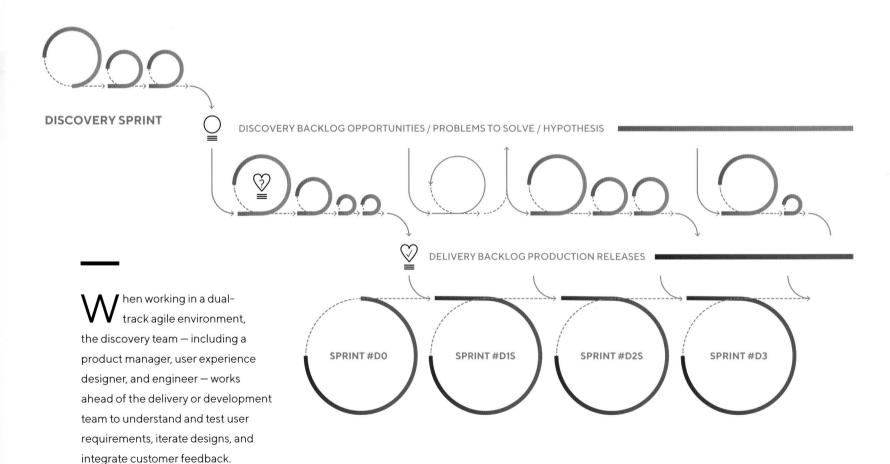

DISCOVERY SPRINT

DISCOVERY BACKLOG OPPORTUNITIES / PROBLEMS TO SOLVE / HYPOTHESIS

DELIVERY BACKLOG PRODUCTION RELEASES

SPRINT #D0   SPRINT #D1S   SPRINT #D2S   SPRINT #D3

When working in a dual-track agile environment, the discovery team — including a product manager, user experience designer, and engineer — works ahead of the delivery or development team to understand and test user requirements, iterate designs, and integrate customer feedback.

Delivering Value and Learning Continuously

In a human-centered organization, exposure is key.

The more exposed stakeholders are to the consumers, the more they will understand them, and the better value they will provide to them. By focusing on uncovering the human problem behind the business problem, the human-centered organization analyzes the experiences offered on the market and seeks to understand what the customers are looking to get done, what pains they must go through, and what gains they are achieving, to provide the best possible solution.

Design's exploratory mindset, abductive thinking, associative processing, and tinkering approach to challenges and opportunities become a facilitator role by:

- Bridging the gap between users and domain subject matter experts
- Articulating technical feasibility and business viability with use value
- Alleviating development and delivery from the stress and cost of testing by quickly prototyping assumptions and hypothesis
- Helping the organization learn continuously and adapt quickly to market changes.

DESIGN FOSTERS INNOVATION AND SUCCESS

The Industry Impact

When design principles are applied to strategy and innovation, the success rate for innovation dramatically improves. For example, on Netflix, 80% or more of the programming that viewers select is now based on algorithmic recommendations.

According to Parsons New School, 71% of organizations that practice design thinking report it has improved their working culture on a team level. Further, 69% of design-led firms perceive the innovation process to be more efficient with design-thinking.

Based on research conducted by Design Council, design can directly and significantly improve sales, profits, turnover, and growth. Using and valuing design brings bottom-line benefits, and those who understand and act on this insight have a competitive edge over the rest.

For example:

- **Rapidly growing businesses are nearly six times as likely as static ones to see design as integral.**
- **Businesses that add value through design see a greater impact on business performance than the rest.**

Companies win market share through design and creativity.

Design helps build an emotional bond with customers.

Market leadership and position are strengthened by design thinking.

"Shares in **design-led businesses** have **outperformed** the FTSE 100 by more than **200%** over the past decade."

HUMANIZING EXPERIENCES

—

Inspiring Trust in Machines
and Humans

BUILDING AN EMOTIONAL CONNECTION WITH CONSUMERS IN THE DIGITAL AGE

Why the Human Touch Matters Now More Than Ever

Machine learning and AI
make the insights of big
data actionable and allow
companies to better respond
to customers in a personal and
relevant way.

Consumer frustration
occurs when companies and
technology fail to provide
personalized experiences.

MAKING OUR DIGITAL CONNECTIONS MORE HUMAN

Machines can now help scale interaction between businesses and their customers. But do they inspire trust, and if so, how?

The ability to interact with another person or in a group is innately human. Personalization, or the custom tailoring of messages or offers to individuals based on their actual behavior, is considered the Holy Grail of the digital world. By connecting with customers' personal tastes, businesses can drive growth, especially in a marketplace where decisions are made in a few seconds.

For a business, responding to curated, personalized experiences means mapping to infinite customer journeys, which becomes impossible without machine learning. Machine learning and AI make the insights of big data actionable and allow companies to better respond to customers in a personal and relevant way.

Consumers have expressed their frustration when companies fail to provide relevant personalized experiences, especially after "intelligent services" such as Amazon's Echo or Google Home digital voice assistants came into the marketplace.

Voice assistants and their continued innovation will go a long way toward alleviating this frustration. Voice assistants like Amazon's Alexa are getting smarter, enabling them to help streamline the purchasing journey for consumers. The idea of relieving a consumer from having to re-create work that's already been completed will go far in establishing and building relationships that create strong brands, loyalty, and lifetime value.

There is nothing more human than getting sick and needing care. With digital technology on the rise, and the increasing cost of health care, everyone recognizes the need to improve access to quality health care and resources for patients. Health care can be confusing and intimidating, and for patients, a "digital front door" represents a friendly, approachable tool that guides patients to better understand a health system's offerings.

Enter GYANT, a startup that brings technology and medical providers together to tackle primary care. The company offers an artificial intelligence-powered chatbot that helps patients get the help they need. Chatbots enable patients to enter information, then receive questions based on symptoms. At the end of the session, the bot can provide the user with information about their condition and potential next steps, including where to turn for appointments and more help.

GYANT was originally trained on three million EHR physician diagnoses, then combined with the patient exchange interactions on the system since 2016. "We want to use AI to improve a provider's ability to diagnose consistently and accurately, see more patients, and, most importantly, help their patients get the care they need," said Pascal Zuta, GYANT CEO. AI-based triage bots will be the new standard for accessing care in the near future. Bots will be able to efficiently triage and process a large number of everyday requests currently handled by over-worked physicians, nurses, and staff, allowing providers to spend more quality time with their patients needing attention and care.

Health Care

"We want to use AI to improve a provider's ability to diagnose consistently and accurately, see more patients, and, most importantly, help their patients get the care they need."

Pascal Zuta,
GYANT CEO

MACHINES HAVE A HARDER TIME DEALING WITH THE SOFTER SIDE OF HUMAN INTERACTION

Why It's Important

The next evolution is emerging from a perception of the value of time spent on digital products. People are realizing that, as they use more digital products and services, they feel they have less time for themselves. They are looking for ways to reduce the time they spend on daily tasks and on their devices.

—

Immediacy and accuracy
are fundamental to personal
experiences.

—

Machines struggle with the
human dimensions of digital
interaction.

6

Benefits

Businesses need to better understand their customers and deliver to them a more personalized experience. Getting to know customers is fundamental to building and fortifying stronger connections.

POTENTIAL OF PERSONALIZATION

REVENUE 5 – 15 %

ACQUISITION COSTS 50 %

MARKETING EFFICIENCY 10 – 30 %

According to McKinsey

PERSONALIZED EXPERIENCES DELIVER TANGIBLE BUSINESS BENEFITS

THE HUMAN STEP IS ALWAYS PART OF THE DIGITAL CHANNEL

2

Connect the dots

- Do not rely on transactional data to draw conclusions. Observe as empirically as possible.

Start small

- Focus on areas of friction. Solve with consistency between experience and brand. Develop design systems to repeat approaches that worked and proven visual and UX elements.

Apply Artificial Intelligence components

- Enrich personalization only when the risk of error is low. Make sure you A/B test when you're leveraging AI, as it can be a double-edged sword that you don't fully control.

Trust the data

- Having good data is absolutely essential. Ask lots of questions, challenge perceptions, and go with your gut, but all of this should be informed by battle-tested and battle-trusted data.

Bring everybody onboard

- Your internal teams and your technology partners need to buy into the level of personalization that needs to be achieved. It can be an upside for them to work it into their internal team incentive levers.

"By 2020, **customer experience** will overtake price and product as the **key brand differentiator**."

According to Frost & Sullivan

Personalization helps
companies understand what
consumers want and design
new products that address
future needs.

Reasons to Believe

The foundation of personalization is
acting on behavioral data.

Personalization can help companies better understand what their customers need and design new products and services for the future that address those needs. There is an ongoing process to validate and test the design of new products, all the while maintaining realistic goals and objectives about what can be delivered at scale.

According to Forrester, to create richer, more relevant experiences for customers, 89% of digital businesses are investing in personalization. Additionally, a more user-centric Internet has led to consumers demanding richer, more interactive experiences. Data mining and predictive analytics can enable companies to create more customization in the form of Internet pages while optimizing Internet searches and tailored offerings.

PERSONALIZATION IS GROUNDED IN BEHAVIORAL DATA

Behavioral Segmentation Methods

to Understand Your Customers

PURCHASING BEHAVIOR

BENEFITS SOUGHT

CUSTOMER USER STAGE

USAGE BASED

OCCASION OR TIMING

CUSTOMER SATISFACTION

CUSTOMER LOYALTY

INTERESTED BASED

ENGAGEMENT LEVEL

USER STATUS

Sets of Personal Data

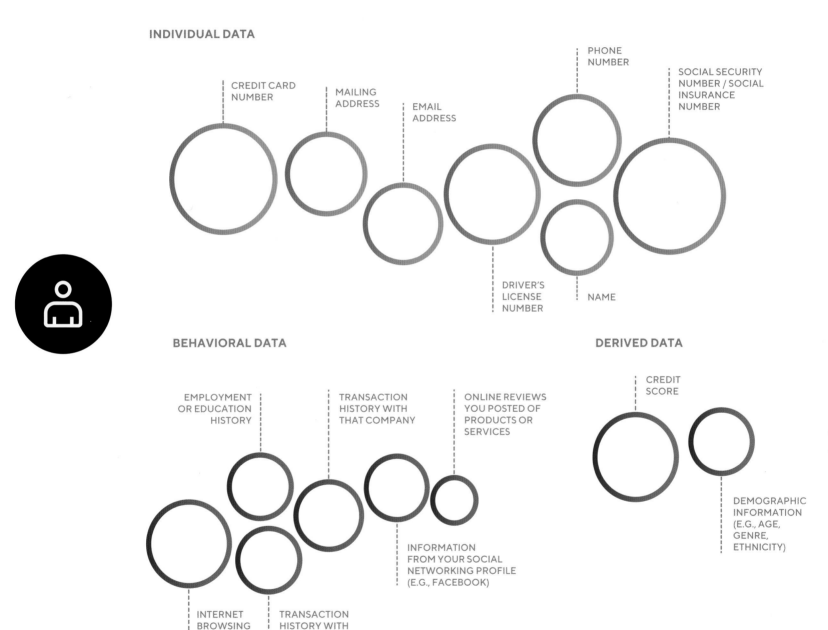

INDIVIDUAL DATA

CREDIT CARD NUMBER

MAILING ADDRESS

EMAIL ADDRESS

PHONE NUMBER

SOCIAL SECURITY NUMBER / SOCIAL INSURANCE NUMBER

DRIVER'S LICENSE NUMBER

NAME

BEHAVIORAL DATA

EMPLOYMENT OR EDUCATION HISTORY

TRANSACTION HISTORY WITH THAT COMPANY

ONLINE REVIEWS YOU POSTED OF PRODUCTS OR SERVICES

INTERNET BROWSING HISTORY

TRANSACTION HISTORY WITH OTHER COMPANIES

INFORMATION FROM YOUR SOCIAL NETWORKING PROFILE (E.G., FACEBOOK)

DERIVED DATA

CREDIT SCORE

DEMOGRAPHIC INFORMATION (E.G., AGE, GENRE, ETHNICITY)

THE ERA OF ONE-ON-ONE

The Industry Impact

The digital road ahead predicts that personalization on all kinds of mobile devices and computing platforms will only increase and intensify. As companies embrace one-on-one personalization, individual consumers will gravitate toward experiences where their interests and preferences are emphasized. Eighty percent of consumers are more likely to do business with a company if it offers a personalized experience, according to Epsilon Research. But businesses will need to strike a balance, because too much personalization can worry customers.

Today's digital businesses are not chasing competition, but rather the expectations of the end consumer. Evolving their approach to personalization — an approach focused on individuals — will help them win.

—

Devise new strategies to capture users' attention, formed with all kinds of personalization.

"80% of consumers are more likely to do business with a company if it offers a **personalized experience**."

According to Epsilon Research

HOW WE START: DATA FIRST

Personalization requires two key elements: knowledge of the person in play and a broad set of peer knowledge into which that person can be mapped.

In a commerce setting, this might be applied to a product recommendation engine, while from a content perspective, this could translate into suggesting news articles.

This peer knowledge is data that can be digested and used to train a machine learning system.

Gather Data

Raw data is gathered regarding who buys or reads what, along with information about those items consumed, and data about those individuals.

Gather Knowledge

In this categorization piece, humans need to define the building blocks that comprise the models the machine learning systems produce.

Design/UI/UX

Ensure the most suitable architectural solution. This involves everything from interaction (voice, app, visual, etc.) to design of the overall architecture of the machine learning system.

Refine

Last, improve the system accuracy, which feeds back into Steps 2 and 3, and may result in tweaks to the model and the machine learning architecture.

Run

Exercise the model and gather KPIs about efficacy and validity, which feeds back into Step 1, and generates more data.

WHY FAIL FAST, AND HOW

—

Quick Wins and
Quick Failures

BOLD APPROACHES TO DETERMINE PRODUCT AND STRATEGIC VIABILITY

Detecting Issues Early to Empower Staff, Systems, and Processes

TRANSFORMATIONS START WITH SMALL, QUICK WINS AND CHEAP, QUICK FAILURES

——

Quickly test and either prove
or disprove digital worthiness.

——

Iteratively embrace end
users through the design and
development process.

——

Ensure that design and
development produce the
best experience.

E merging technologies and design approaches are a dynamic part of digital transformations. Being able to quickly test and either prove or disprove their worthiness is central to moving projects and partnerships forward.

The educational testing nonprofit ACT was founded in 1959 and has made a clear decision to transform the way they run their business and engage with stakeholders. As an example, it developed and launched ACT Academy, which is designed to help students improve their college and career readiness by leveraging video lessons, interactive practice questions, full-length practice tests, educational games, and other materials targeted to their academic needs.

The primary benefit is digital products that are innovative and that are embraced by end users quickly. Take, for example, the testing company designing and building applications for test administrators to check students into the exam, manage the testing venue, and administer tests at scale (hundreds of students per venue, millions nationally). Imperative to success is the ability to pilot quickly in a real test environment, learn, and prioritize the product backlog immediately. This sets up an established paper-based process to be disrupted and embraced by users with tablets. It is the fastest path to removing friction in the business.

Why It's Important

By working through quick wins or failures with a discovery process, business stakeholders and partners can experiment and test emerging technologies quickly and efficiently.

IT DOESN'T WORK UNTIL IT DOES. USERS AND MARKET CONTEXT CANNOT BE ARTIFICIAL

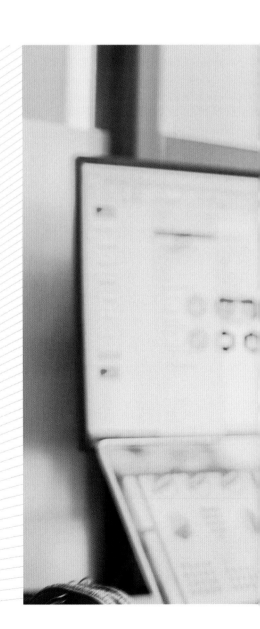

Experiment and test emerging technologies quickly and effectively.

Partners are inextricably linked to the overall discovery process.

Engagement with stakeholders is affected.

SCALE WHAT WORKS. TURN OFF WHAT DOESN'T

There are many benefits to "failing fast," including saving time and money. Failing fast also enables companies and individuals to be in a stronger position to focus on projects that are experiencing success.

One additional benefit to failing fast is that it allows companies to quickly pivot and make adjustments based on what the user wants or uncovers as a new feature.

But not enough can be said for the process of failure and what it teaches. Failing leads to experimentation, and the idea of experimenting breeds learning. This iterative learning process provides short-term gains and yields long-term advantages as well, including teaching how to adapt to a particular environment. This adaptation helps build skills and momentum for future scenarios and business cases. In turn, this learning can be shared with coworkers, partners, and others who are part of the cocreation process.

YOUR DESIGN SYSTEM MUST ALWAYS LEARN

1. Evaluate Opportunities

Understand pain points and gaps by breaking down the tasks users want to complete and creating critical user flows.

2. Wireframe/Design Concepts

Create clickable prototypes based on critical user flows to bring the most compelling experiences to life.

3. Rapid Prototyping

Prototype only the ideas necessary to have a better understanding of the problem space and answer questions.

4. Usability Feedback

See how users react and interact with the prototypes to understand which route to take with the product.

Pilot quickly and learn in a real test environment.

Achieve a faster path to reduce digital friction points.

CREATING A COLLABORATIVE DIALOGUE OPEN TO NEW IDEAS

Building a culture of
continued user feedback
is crucial.

Prototype, Test, and Learn

- Structure your pod team with strong product leadership and mindset. This naturally enables the pod to connect to users.
- Build a nurturing environment that encourages a continuous and open dialogue.
- Embrace experimentation in your culture.

Embed New and Emerging Tools

- Use tools to enable agility (InVision and other prototyping tools, videos of screens showing functionality). All of these make proof of concepts cheap, iterative, and fast, and elicit real-time feedback that directly impacts the product backlog and road map.

It's Never Too Late for New Ideas

- New ideas are the lifeblood of any business and brand, and new ideas can be revealed at any time during the business process and team collaboration.
- New ideas can be tied to new user insights, technologies, markets, products, geographical preferences, among others. Embrace the new idea and its inspiration.

Fail Fast, Early, and Cheap

- Fail fast, early, and as cheaply as possible.
- Be sure to test concepts and different approaches, and learn from early test phases.
- Adapt new models and learning to elicit the right emotional and rational results.

REINVENTION MUST BE IN THE CULTURE

By 2021, more than 1.8 billion people will be using voice digital assistants. Voice is projected to drive over $11.7 billion in business to consumer revenue. Due to this growth, voice may be a technology worth experimenting in, to identify areas where it may impact business.

With tools like Siri shortcuts or the simple creation of a prototype Alexa or Google Home app, organizations can experiment in these areas quickly and test their potential impact by collaborating with internal stakeholders.

On the consumer-facing side, brands may need to treat investments in this area with a level of urgency because of both the nature of voice's efficiency and the behemoths in control of the interfaces.

Amazon's Alexa, for example, will efficiently take a consumer to the most appropriate product, selected by its algorithm, with very little control or sway afforded to the various sellers of that product category. That could be a serious problem as the usage of voice grows and competition mounts. Brands need to make themselves top-of-mind to be called out by name at home, and there needs to be a strategy to prevent being locked out by personal assistants' algorithms.

Change requires adaptation.

Be experimental and transparent.

Expect the digital landscape to be shaped continuously.

"The number of **Internet-connected things** will reach 50 billion by 2020, with **$19 trillion in profits** and cost savings coming from IoT over the next decade."

According to CMO by Adobe

Digitalization is transforming the energy industry by improving efficiency and safety, and by facilitating the use of renewable energy.

Digitalization is about more than technology. It is also a cultural change, about people and creating more agile ways of working. The environment in which teams work is critical in framing and enabling the right behaviors and mind-set necessary for the process of co-creation and value delivery.

Shell's digital facility in R&D has been completely transformed into a space that combines lean start-up thinking and design processes. This has helped to break down silos and fuel innovation through rapid experiments and by integrating domain knowledge with digital technology.

As a result, teams are able to ideate, learn (and fail) fast, and drive priorities in a space that accommodates different work styles, all while empowering project teams to deliver effectively.

One of several opportunities to be realized is Shell's application of machine learning and artificial intelligence to improve how drilling teams target wells to pinpoint optimal layers of rock in the earth that contain oil and gas. "Geosteering" is the challenge of pinpointing the long, horizontal well position exactly and steering it to reach the most productive rock containing oil and gas.

Shell developed Shell Geodesic™ to improve the accuracy and consistency of a horizontal well's directional control to reach optimal oil and gas rock. Geodesic streams drilling data and processes algorithms to make real-time decisions that better predict outcomes. It features a drilling simulator, which offers a user-friendly interface and a suite of machine learning and control algorithms that improve performance.

Shell

INNOVATION FUNNEL

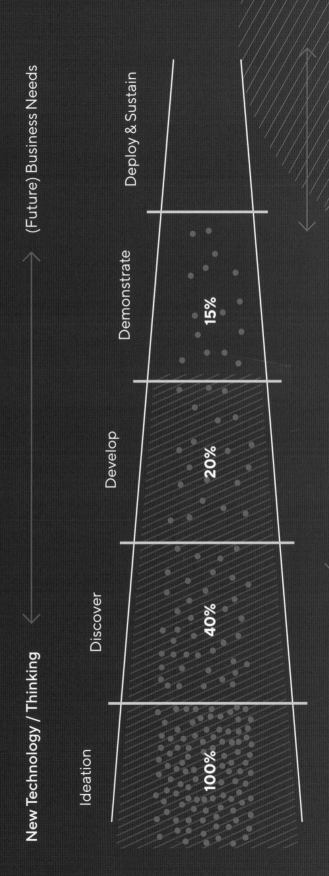

New Technology / Thinking → (Future) Business Needs

Ideation

Discover

Develop

Demonstrate

Deploy & Sustain

100%

40%

20%

15%

Digital Development Team

REIMAGINE YOUR BUSINESS PRAGMATICALLY; EXPERIMENT CONTINUOUSLY

The Industry Impact

The future holds a great deal of new, emerging technologies that will shape and reshape the digital landscape. In order to be a digital leader in the industry, organizations must foster a culture that embraces two principles: be highly collaborative and experiment.

Another suggestion to enable a culture of experimentation is the idea of having a small team that can deliver "labs" engagements. It may be a team of two to three people who move quickly to identify and prove (or disprove) ideas. See the graphic on the five-week engagement with a large well-known fashion retailer on the facing page.

Rather than investing in hardware for all of our stores ... can we get customers to BYOD (Bring Your Own Device) for requesting new sizes from the dressing room?

5 weeks to pilot

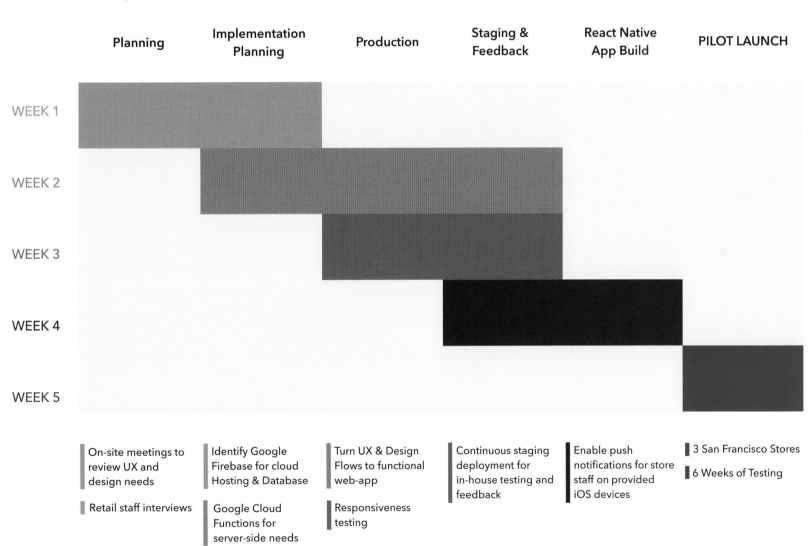

	Planning	Implementation Planning	Production	Staging & Feedback	React Native App Build	PILOT LAUNCH
WEEK 1						
WEEK 2						
WEEK 3						
WEEK 4						
WEEK 5						

On-site meetings to review UX and design needs

Retail staff interviews

Identify Google Firebase for cloud Hosting & Database

Google Cloud Functions for server-side needs

Turn UX & Design Flows to functional web-app

Responsiveness testing

Continuous staging deployment for in-house testing and feedback

Enable push notifications for store staff on provided iOS devices

3 San Francisco Stores

6 Weeks of Testing

CHANGE IS THE ONLY INVARIANT

—

Final Takeaways

Companies and business and technology executives are under extreme pressure to address a growing set of challenges:

- Lack of a coherent plan and digitization strategy
- Limited resources
- Employee resistance
- Lack of talent and expertise to lead a digital initiative
- Organizational structure that's more obstacle than opportunity

At times like these, and to bring a bit of levity to the situation, it helps to turn our attention to a pop culture icon for a bit of level-setting and perhaps inspiration.

In the somewhat forgettable movie *Road House*, which came out thirty years ago, Patrick Swayze plays Dalton, a bouncer with a PhD and a Zen-like philosophy, who's been hired to clean up a mean, rowdy bar. When asked how he's handling the new job, his response is, "Nothing I ain't used to. But it's amazing what you can get used to." Dalton is, in essence, all of us when it comes to digital transformation.

To be successful today, companies and those responsible for leading the digital transformation charge need to operate in a world and with a mindset where innovation and transformation are continuous.

If no one has said it directly, allow me to be the first. You will never be fully and finally transformed. You don't get to cross the finish line. You will always be transforming.

Forrester recently surveyed more than 1,500 business and technology decision-makers, and the results revealed a troubling message of reluctance to change. Twenty-one percent of survey respondents thought they were finished with their transformation. We need to understand and, in many respects, embrace the idea that digital transformation is an ongoing process.

The best and most successful companies not only understand this, but embrace the opportunity it provides them.

Which, of course, brings us back to the purpose behind this book, and that's that transformation really shouldn't happen in a vacuum. Companies at every stage of the transformation game need partners that will help them understand the necessary steps that are critical to realizing success and making the most out of this experience.

"AGILE" THEORY DOES NOT HELP

Any agile implementation needs to fit your needs, rather than prescribe artificial processes or practices that don't make sense for your business. If speed, team autonomy, quality, and business outcomes don't emerge, whoever is leading your agile transformation is underperforming. Make sure you measure what matters to your business.

+ CHAPTER 3 & 4

YES, FAIL FAST, BUT LEARN AS WELL, AND DO IT AS CHEAPLY AS YOU CAN

It's only failure if you don't learn and take nothing away. Set objectives at the outset and ensure that the organization and stakeholders get smarter every step of the way.

+ CHAPTER 7

GO LEAN, AND GO ACROSS

Design thinking and agile methodologies are hallmarks of a lean organization and help advance collaboration and talent development. You may not be able to knock down all your silos to increase speed, but at a minimum, you may build bridges across them. Podification can help you get started quickly and show quick wins that trigger larger improvements as you show progress.

+ CHAPTER 3 & 5

PERSONALIZATION IS MANDATORY

Customers at every level expect a personal experience on their journey, regardless of whether it's in-store, through a virtual assistant, or on their mobile device. If you don't give it to them, they will surely get it from someone else.

+ CHAPTER 6

PARTNERS CAN ACCELERATE GROWTH IF YOU KNOW HOW TO INCENTIVIZE THEM TO BUILD JOINT VALUE

As new technologies and faster pace and execution approaches become the norm, staying ahead of the game without specialized help is too difficult. Take a more serious view of your partner ecosystem, pick the right technology partners, and consider them an integral part of your execution strategy. Assess your partnerships for achieving your business outcomes and be serious about sharing upside. Incentivize a healthy, leveled relationship where you recognize, select, and constantly assess the value and culture that you need in order to lead in the market.

+ CHAPTER 1

ALL ABOUT THE PEOPLE

Acquiring, training, and retaining the talent that you need to achieve the outcomes your business needs to thrive requires that you put effort in building community.

+ CHAPTER 2

AND ALL ABOUT THE DATA

It's not too late to become a data-driven organization. Technologies like AI and machine learning will continue to make your data smarter and add velocity to customer identification and experiences.

+ CHAPTER 6

TRANSFORM WHILE YOU PERFORM

Business doesn't stop. Today's environment demands that we digitally transform today while we continue to perform.

APPENDICES

—

Glossary
Sources
Acknowledgments
About the Author

GLOSSARY

A

Agile Software Development
A set of fundamental principles about how software should be developed based on an agile way of working, in contrast to previous heavy-handed software development methodologies.

Agile Teams
These teams have the autonomy to work the way its members like to work. They build mastery as a team and take roles when needed to serve the higher purpose.

Autonomy
A group's right to self-government or self-rule. When a person seeks autonomy, he or she would like to be able to make decisions independently from an authority figure.

Backlog

A collection of stories and tasks the sprint team will work on at some point in the future. Either the product owner has not prioritized them or has assigned them lower priority.

Build Process

The amount of variability in implementation makes it difficult to come up with a tight definition of a build process, but we would say that a build process takes source code and other configuration data as input and produces artifacts (sometimes called derived objects) as output. The exact number and definition of steps depends greatly on the types of inputs (Java versus C/C++ versus Perl/Python/Ruby source code) and the type of desire output (CD image, downloadable zip file, self-extracting binary, etc.). When the source code includes a compiled language, then the build process would certainly include a compilation and perhaps a linking step.

Business Process Modeling (BPM)

The activity of representing processes of an enterprise, so that the current ("as is") process may be analyzed and improved in future ("to be").

Capability Maturity Model (CMM)

In software engineering, CMM is a model of the maturity of the capability of certain business processes. A maturity model can be described as a structured collection of elements that describe certain aspects of maturity in an organization and aids in the definition and understanding of an organization's processes.

Change Management

A field of management focused on organizational changes that aims to ensure that methods and procedures are used for efficient and prompt handling of all changes to controlled IT infrastructure in order to minimize the number and impact of any related incidents upon service.

Communities

A group of people having a particular characteristic in common, defined as a body of persons of common and especially professional interests scattered through a larger society.

Core Members

At the center of our pods are these outstanding individuals who have the technical skills combined with soft and leadership skills, and who fully understand the client's domain.

Cost Engineering

The area of engineering practice where engineering judgment and experience are used in the application of scientific principles and techniques to problems of cost estimating, cost control, business planning and management science, profitability analysis, project management, and planning and scheduling.

Cross-Functional Teams

Teams comprised of several different skill sets and capabilities.

Cross-Pollination

Bringing various types of talented people together, allowing their knowledge and skills to influence each other. Cross-pollination can expose employees to different ideas and new ways of thinking.

Design

A plan or drawing produced to show the look and function or workings of a building, garment, or other object before it is built or made.

Design Thinking

Refers to the cognitive, strategic, and practical processes by which design concepts (proposals for new products, buildings, machines, etc.) are developed by designers and/or design teams. Many of the key concepts and aspects of design thinking have been identified through studies of design cognition and design activity across different design domains, in both laboratory and natural contexts.

Design System

A design system is a series of components that can be reused in different combinations. Design systems allow you to manage design at scale.

Development Framework

A platform for developing software applications that provides a foundation on which software developers can build programs. It involves a basic conceptual structure used to solve or address complex issues in software projects, typically a set of tools, materials, or components. By applying and enforcing the use of these reusable components and templates with review processes, the risk of inconsistent delivery is reduced.

DevOps

The clipped compound of "development" and "operations" is a software development method that stresses communication, collaboration, integration, automation, and measurement of cooperation between software developers and other information-technology (IT) professionals.

Digital Journey

A context-aware interaction between an end user and a brand or business whereby the interaction becomes a digital conversation in which technology establishes and builds a powerful experience with deep emotional connections through three key values: simplification, surprise, and anticipation.

Digital Native

A person or a company born in the digital era and defined by their approach to technology that embraces a lean software practice willing to try, fail, and try again with an entrepreneurial startup.

Digital Revolution

The shift from mechanical and analog electronic technology to digital electronics, which began between the late 1950s and the late 1970s with the adoption and proliferation of digital computers and digital record-keeping that continues to the present day.

Digital Transformation

The novel use of digital technology to solve traditional problems. These digital solutions enable inherently new types of innovation and creativity, rather than simply enhancing and supporting traditional methods.

Efficiency

Signifies a level of performance that uses the least amount of input to achieve the highest amount of output. It requires reducing the number of unnecessary resources used to produce a given output, including personal time and energy.

Fourth Industrial Revolution

The fourth major industrial era since the initial Industrial Revolution of the eighteenth century. It is characterized by a fusion of technologies that blurs the lines between the physical, digital,

and biological spheres, collectively referred to as cyber-physical systems.

Framework
An abstraction in which software providing generic functionality can be selectively changed by additional user-written code, thus providing application-specific software. A software framework provides a standard way to build and deploy applications.

Game of Pods
A gamification approach that integrates pods and communities and helps model behavior, with a bottom-up, empowering direction, by rewarding both collective and individual contribution.

Gamification
The application of typical elements of game-playing (e.g. point-scoring, competition with others, rules of play) to other areas of activity to encourage engagement with a product or service. The approach and process of creating a game environment and then utilizing gaming technologies to boost and improve the overall productivity of developer teams. By doing so, team members can collaborate and bridge divisions between creative and engineering teams and establish a richer, more flexible integration of varied technology skill sets.

Governance Model
The action, manner of applying a set of pre-established criteria for monitoring, measuring, and managing the software development life cycle. These frameworks reflect the interrelated relationships, factors, and other influences involved in a software development project.

Guilds
An association of people for mutual aid or the pursuit of a common goal.

Innovation
The introduction of something new; a new idea, method, or device.

Iteration
A period, from one week to two months in duration, during which the agile development team produces an increment of completed software. All system life cycle phases (requirements, design, code, and test) must be completed during the iteration and then empirically demonstrated for the iteration to be accepted as successfully completed. At the beginning of the iteration, the business or product owner identifies the next (highest-priority) chunk of work for the team to complete. The development team then estimates the level of effort and commits to completing a segment of work during the iteration. During the iteration,

the team is not expected to change objectives or respond to change requests. However, at the front end of the next iteration, the business or product owner is free to identify any new segment of work as the current highest priority.

Iterative and Incremental Development

A cyclic software development process developed in response to the weaknesses of the waterfall model. It starts with initial planning and ends with deployment with the cyclic interaction in between.

Kanban

A tool derived from lean manufacturing associated with the branch of agile practices loosely referred to as lean software development. Like a task board, Kanban visually represents the state of work in process. Unlike a task board, the Kanban constrains how much work in process is permitted to occur at the same time. The purpose of limiting work in process is to reduce bottlenecks and increase throughput by optimizing that segment of the value stream that is the subject of the Kanban. A principal difference between Kanban and Scrum is that Scrum limits work in process through timeboxing (i.e. the sprint) and Kanban limits work in process by limiting how much work may occur at one time (e.g. *n* tasks or *n* stories).

KPI

A performance indicator or key performance indicator is a type of performance measurement. KPIs evaluate the success of an organization or of a particular activity in which it engages.

Maturity Path

A maturity assessment to identify gaps between the current and future state. This assessment informs a path where you can make improvements over time to create an improved landscape.

Mozilla

Mozilla was Netscape Communication's nickname for Navigator, its first Web browser, and the name of an open-source public collaboration created to develop Navigator. AOL acquired Netscape in 1998 and stopped supporting the browser in 2008. The ongoing Mozilla Foundation's main focus is the Firefox browser.

Netflix

Netflix, Inc. is an American media-services provider headquartered California. The company's primary business is its subscription-based streaming OTT service which offers online streaming of a library of films and television programs, including those produced in-house.

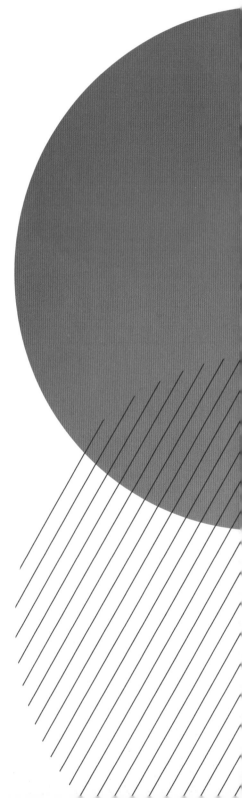

Outcome
Something that follows as a result or consequence.

Pods
A system and approach that provides companies and organizations with a cohesive way to design and build products.

Pods Formula
Using a pod where leveraging of digital technologies helps create new business models, revenue streams, and a method to address the changing business environment and market dynamics.

Pods Framework
A group of pods that connects different functional groups within the business so that a single team can own the delivery of a digital product.

Pod Template Compliance
A pod template defines the composition of a pod in terms of roles and specific experience. Each pod type (solution, development, evolution, DevOps) has an associated template. This is done to make sure guidelines are followed and that there's a balanced set of roles. For example, a solutions pod needs to have product and design roles, as described in the template. If a solutions pod is weak in design, then it will not be compliant with the solution pod template.

Podification
The application of pods being leveraged across business groups or an enterprise to provide efficiency and scale in those projects.

Podify
The action and benefits derived from applying pod methods and practices across a business unit, organization, or enterprise.

Predictability
Consistent repetition of a state, course of action, behavior, or the like, making it possible to know in advance what to expect.

Product Impact
Aims to improve understanding of how users change in the process of interaction with products, and to integrate this knowledge in design practice.

Project Accounting
The practice of creating financial reports specifically designed to track the financial progress of projects, which can then be used by managers to aid project management.

Project Cost Management

A method of managing a project in real time from the estimating stage to project control through the use of technology, cost, schedule, and monitoring productivity.

Project Management Software

A type of software, including scheduling, cost control and budget management, resource allocation, collaboration software, communication, quality management, and documentation or administration systems, which are used to deal with the complexity of large projects.

Quality

The standard of something as measured against other things of a similar kind.

Retention

The continued possession, use, or control of something in a pod or pod framework.

Seniority Ratio

The percentage of experienced pod members who are considered "senior." Seniority is generally defined by the number of years of experience in technology or management positions. This differs from "core member ratio," as core members are those who have specific experience in being part of a pod and working within the context of one or more digital journeys for a client.

Scrum

A set of practices used in agile project management that emphasize daily communication and the flexible reassessment of plans that are carried out in short, iterative phases of work.

SME

Subject Matter Experts, people who have special skills or knowledge on a particular job or topic.

Spotify

A digital music service that enables users to remotely source millions of songs or various "record labels" from a laptop, smartphone, or other device.

Sprint

The scrum term for an iteration. The sprint starts with a sprint planning meeting. At the end of the sprint, there is a sprint review meeting, followed by a sprint retrospective meeting.

Story

A requirement, feature, and/or unit of business value that can be estimated and tested. Stories describe work that must be done to create and deliver a feature for a product. Stories are the basic unit of communication, planning, and negotiation between the scrum team, business owners, and the product owner. Stories consist of the following elements: a description, usually in business terms; a size, for rough estimation purposes, generally expressed in story points (such as 1, 2, 3, 4); and an acceptance test, giving a short description of how the story will be validated.

Story Point

The story-point unit of measurement describes a user scenario that involves some kind of interaction between some form of software and a user, or another system. Sizing product features in story points helps a pod estimate product size, complexity, and its derivatives, such as velocity and cost.

Studios

A physical space that gathers a variety of technology, design, and business talents with specific skill sets and areas of expertise that are integrated into pod methods, structures, and outputs.

Talent
Natural aptitude or skill.

Transformational Partnerships
An alliance among two or more interested parties in a common enterprise, where each partner brings its own interests, competencies, and resources, which they combine to achieve a shared development goal, measured against defined results.

Value Partnership
A partnership that is innovation-driven, distributed, and highly participatory.

Velocity
Measures how much work a team can complete in an iteration. Velocity is often measured in stories or story points, but could also measure tasks in hours or an equivalent unit. Velocity is used to measure how long it will take a particular team to deliver future outcomes by extrapolating on the basis of its prior performance. This works in agile development, when work is comprehensively completed after each iteration.

Uberization
The conversion of existing jobs and services into discrete tasks that can be requested on demand. The term has been adopted from the business model and technology practices of the taxi service Uber.

WGLL
Or "What Good Looks Like."

Value-Add
The amount by which the value of an article is increased at each stage of its production, exclusive of initial costs.

SOURCES

INTRODUCTION

Thomas Davenport and George Westerman, "Why So Many High-Profile Digital Transformations Fail," *Harvard Business Review*, March 2018

Rosabeth Moss Kanter, "Collaborative Advantage: The Art of Alliances," *Harvard Business Review*, July 1994

Robert Parker and Shawn Fitzgerald, " IDC FutureScape: Worldwide Digital Transformation 2018 Predictions," IDC, November 2017, https://www.idc.com/getdoc.jsp?containerId=US43234117

Noam Wasserman, *The Founder's Dilemma* (Princeton, New Jersey: Princeton University Press, 2012)

CHAPTER 1

Benjamin Gomes-Casseres, "Partnership is Not a Purchase Order," *Harvard Business Review,* May 16, 2011, https://hbr.org/2011/05/partnership-not-purchase-order

"2018 U.S. Online Retail Forecast," FTI Consulting, September 10, 2018, https://www.fticonsulting.com/insights/articles/2018-us-online-retail-forecast

Ray Zinn, "Tech Partnership Strategies," Forbes Technology Council, *Forbes*, January 2018, https://www.forbes.com/sites/forbestechcouncil/2018/01/11/tech-partnership-strategies/#67fba31840f0

CHAPTER 2

Mitchell Baker, "What is the Role of Mozilla's Executive Chair?" Lizard Wrangling, May 27, 2016, https://blog.lizardwrangler.com/2016/05/27/what-is-the-role-of-mozillas-executive-chair/

Denelle Dixon, "The Power of Mozilla," Mozilla, December 8, 2025, https://blog.mozilla.org/blog/2015/12/08/the-power-of-mozilla/

Gartner, "Successfully Source Digital Talent," https://www.gartner.com/en/human-resources/insights/talent-in-digital

Mozilla, https://www.mozilla.org/en-US/mission/

Mozilla, https://www.mozilla.org/en-US/about/governance/

Mozilla Community Program, https://wiki.mozilla.org/Community:CommunityProgram

CHAPTER 3

Ranjona Banerji, "How Foursquare, Netflix & Spotify are developing agile organizations," MxM, Media Marketing More, October 15, 2013, http://www.mxmindia.com/2013/10/how-foursquare-netflix-spotify-are-developing-agile-organizations/

Norberts Erts, "What are the benefits of an agile organization?" Cake HR, September 16, 2018, https://blog.cake.hr/agile-organizations-are-agile-organisation-models-the-future/

Forrester, "Predictions 2019: Transformation Goes Pragmatic," https://go.forrester.com/blogs/predictions-2019-transformation-goes-pragmatic/

Michael Mankins and Eric Garton, "How Spotify Balances Employee Autonomy and Accountability," *Harvard Business Review*, February 9, 2017, https://hbr.org/2017/02/how-spotify-balances-employee-autonomy-and-accountability

CHAPTER 4

Anita Ann Babu, "Gamification and Your LMS: 3 Trends You Should Know About," Software Advice, https://www.softwareadvice.com/resources/gamification-trends-for-lms/

John Brandon, "3 Enterprise Gamification Success Stories," CIO, March 23, 2015, https://www.cio.com/article/2900319/3-enterprise-gamification-success-stories.html

"Gamification Market — Growth, Trends, and Forecast (2019 – 2024)," Mordor Intelligence, https://www.mordorintelligence.com/industry-reports/gamification-market

"State of the Global Workplace," Gallup, https://www.gallup.com/services/178517/state-global-workplace.aspx

Chris Tuff, "New Book Shows Companies How to Effectively Recruit, Retain, & Motivate Millennials," Cision PR Newswire, February 11, 2019, https://www.prnewswire.com/news-releases/new-book-shows-companies-how-to-effectively-recruit-retain--motivate-millennials-300792056.html

CHAPTER 5

Giselle Abramovich, "Design-Led Businesses Do These Three Things Right," CMO, June 9, 2017, http://www.cmo.com/features/articles/2017/5/22/study-finds-designled-businesses-do-these-three-things-tlp-cc-ddm.html

Rafiq Elmansy, "Ideation in Design Thinking: Tools and Method," Designorate, May 2, 2017, https://www.designorate.com/ideation-design-thinking-tools/

Tony Harmer, "4 Key Stats on the Importance of Design for Business," Creative Connection, October 14, 2015, https://blogs.adobe.com/creative/design-advantage/

Katrina Lake, "Stitch Fix's CEO on Selling Personal Style to the Mass Market," *Harvard Business Review*, from the May–June 2018 issue, https://hbr.org/2018/05/stitch-fixs-ceo-on-selling-personal-style-to-the-mass-market

Netflix, www.netflix.com

"New Study on Design Thinking Adoption in Organizations," The New School Parsons, http://sds.parsons.edu/designmanagement/new-study-on-design-thinking/

Stitch Fix, "This Is Stitch Fix: Your New Way To Shop," https://www.stitchfix.com/women/blog/inside-stitchfix/stitch-fix-new-way-shop/

"The Value of Design Factfinder Report," Design Council, 2007, https://www.designcouncil.org.uk/sites/default/files/asset/document/TheValueOfDesignFactfinder_Design_Council.pdf

Michael Westcott, "Design-Driven Companies Outperform S&P by 228% Over Ten Years — The 'DMI Design Value Index,'" updated March 10, 2014, https://www.dmi.org/blogpost/1093220/182956/Design-Driven-Companies-Outperform-S-P-by-228-Over-Ten-Years--The-DMI-Design-Value-Index

CHAPTER 6

Erin Dietsche, "This startup leverages AI and providers to focus on primary care," MedCityNews, October 2018, https://medcitynews.com/2018/10/startup-ai-providers-primary-care/

Forrester, Evolve Now to Personalization 2.0: Individualization, December 2017, https://www.forrester.com/report/Evolve+Now+To+Personalization+20+Individualization/-/E-RES11737

"Frost & Sullivan: Omnichannel Customer Experience to Be a Necessity," destinationCRM, July 26, 2016, https://www.destinationcrm.com/Articles/ReadArticle.aspx?ArticleID=112549

Brian Gregg, Hussein Kalaoui, Joel Maynes, and Gustavo Schuler, "Marketing's Holy Grail: Digital personalization at scale," McKinsey Digital, November 2016, https://www.mckinsey.com/business-functions/digital-mckinsey/our-insights/marketings-holy-grail-digital-personalization-at-scale

Laura Lovett, "AI triage chatbots trekking toward a standard of care despite criticism," mobihealthnews, November 2018, https://www.mobihealthnews.com/content/ai-triage-chatbots-trekking-toward-standard-care-despite-criticism

Blake Morgan, "Five Trends Shaping the Future of Customer Experience in 2018," *Forbes*, December 5, 2017, https://www.forbes.com/sites/blakemorgan/2017/12/05/five-trends-shaping-the-future-of-customer-experience-in-2018/#2c2cf4742d9c

"New Epsilon research indicates 80% of consumers are more likely to make a purchase when brands offer personalized experiences," Epsilon, January 9, 2018, http://pressroom.epsilon.com/new-epsilon-research-indicates-80-of-consumers-are-more-likely-to-make-a-purchase-when-brands-offer-personalized-experiences/

"So, what's a 'digital front door'? And why does it matter?" GYANT Blog, https://medium.com/gyant-blog/so-whats-a-digital-front-door-and-why-does-it-matter-f6f4660bc20b

"2018 CX Trends Report," InMoment, February 22, 2018, https://www.inmoment.com/resources/2018-cx-trends-report/

CHAPTER 7

"ACT to Launch ACT Academy, a Free, Online Learning Program Designed to Help Improve ACT Scores, College Readiness," ACT, January 23, 2018, http://leadershipblog.act.org/2018/01/act-to-launch-act-academy-free-online.html

Giselle Abramovich, "15 Mind-Blowing Stats About The Internet of Things," CMO.com, April 17, 2015, https://www.cmo.com/features/articles/2015/4/13/mind-blowing-stats-internet-of-things-iot.html#gs.c34zgs

Stacey Childress, SchoolBoard contributor, "3 Biggest Education Innovation Questions for 2018," *Forbes*, January 8, 2018, https://www.forbes.com/sites/schoolboard/2018/01/08/3-biggest-education-innovation-questions-for-2018/#4045aa704b13

Brian Gregg, Hussein Kalaoui, Joel Maynes, and Gustavo Schuler, "Marketing's Holy Grail: Digital personalization at scale," McKinsey Digital, November 2016, https://www.mckinsey.com/business-functions/digital-mckinsey/our-insights/marketings-holy-grail-digital-personalization-at-scale

Forrester, "Predictions 2019: Transformation Goes Pragmatic," https://go.forrester.com/blogs/predictions-2019-transformation-goes-pragmatic/

FINAL TAKEAWAYS

Forrester, "Predictions 2019: Transformation Goes Pragmatic," https://go.forrester.com/blogs/predictions-2019-transformation-goes-pragmatic/

Forrester, "The Sorry State of Digital Transformation in 2018," April 2018, https://go.forrester.com/blogs/the-sorry-state-of-digital-transformation-in-2018/

ACKNOWLEDGMENTS

Transforming While Performing was a challenging undertaking, from shaping the ideas, words, and illustrations to conveying to our customers, partners, and industries the essence of Cognizant Softvision's approaches in creating partnerships that effect impactful business outcomes in the digital economy. It was a very rewarding process, and I trust readers will enjoy what they find in it as much as we have enjoyed creating it. Like any highly collaborative and creative undertaking, we needed a host of diverse talents from inside and outside of our company to make this book come together. This book would not have been possible without the dedicated and inspiring efforts of many fellow Softvisioners, who I'd like to personally thank for their contributions, including Alejandra Sosa, Bret Cunningham, Bogdan Nicule, David Bolcsfoldi, Eugenio Calamari, Fausta Ballesteros, Ines Casares, Ioana Chiorean, Jim Hartling, Mihai Constandis, Paula Fernández, Ryan Riley, Snjezana Cvoro-Begovic, Forest Carlisle, and many more.

Thanks also to Lee Bruno and Tony Telloni, my partners in writing this book, who worked with us polishing and making sense of every word, putting up with many revisions and changes.

I also deeply thank my wonderful family, my wife, Laura, and our great kids, Emma, Dante, Valentino, and Siena. They supported this effort despite the many weekends and nighttime hours I spent on my laptop and away from home. It has been an exciting ride only possible thanks to their love and support.

Transforming While Performing has been a team effort. It is rewarding and exciting to see how several months of hard work resulted in a book that represents the approach to building a culture of partnership that improves companies' ability to thrive in the Fourth Industrial Revolution.

ABOUT THE AUTHOR

Andres Angelani is the Chief Executive Officer of Cognizant Softvision. He has extensive experience building strategic partnerships that create new revenue streams, realizing innovative business models and market offerings through new ways of developing software, and building high-performance teams and the right culture to bring the best of what design and technology have to offer to industries. Andres is at the epicenter of today's digital economy, leading programs that have reshaped businesses and industries. His passion for music, science, and technology helped shape his life and professional career, and has become an integral part of what he brings to his leadership in fostering innovative culture, inspiring and growing talent in new, transformative ways.

Angelani is a frequent speaker and thought leader. In 2016, he coauthored *The Never-Ending Digital Journey: Creating New Consumer Experiences Through Technology. Transforming While Performing* is his second book.

DISCLAIMER